SEASHELLS IN MY POCKET
Third Edition

About the AMC

What Is the Appalachian Mountain Club?
Since 1876, the Appalachian Mountain Club has been promoting the protection, enjoyment, and wise use of the mountains, rivers, and trails of the Northeast outdoors. We are the nation's oldest outdoor recreation and conservation organization.

Join Us!
Members support our mission while enjoying great AMC activities, our award-winning AMC Outdoors magazine, and special discounts. Join online, or call 800-372-1758 for more information.

People
We are nearly 90,000 members in 12 chapters, 20,000 volunteers, and over 450 full time and seasonal staff. Our chapters reach from Maine to Washington D.C.

Outdoor Fun
We offer over 8,000 trips each year, from local chapter activities to major excursions worldwide, for every ability level and outdoor interest – from hiking and climbing to paddling to snowshoeing and skiing.

Great Places to Stay
We serve over 140,000 guests each year at our AMC Lodges, Huts, Full-Service Camps, Cabins, Shelters and Campgrounds – each AMC Destination is a model for environmental education and stewardship.

Opportunities for Learning
We teach people the skills to be safe outdoors and care for the natural world around us, through programs for children, teens and adults, as well as outdoor leadership training.

Caring for Trails
We maintain over 1,700 miles of trails throughout the Northeast, including nearly 350 miles of the Appalachian Trail in five states.

Protecting Wild Places
We advocate for land and riverway conservation, monitor air quality, and work to protect alpine and forest ecosystems through the Northern Forest and Highlands regions.

Engaging the Public
We seek to educate and inform our own members and an additional 1.5 million people annually through AMC Books, our website, our White Mountain visitor centers, and AMC Destinations.

SEASHELLS IN MY POCKET
Third Edition

AMC's Family Guide to Exploring the Coast
from Maine to Florida

by Judith Hansen
illustrated by Donna Sabaka

APPALACHIAN MOUNTAIN CLUB BOOKS
BOSTON, MASSACHUSETTS

The AMC is a non-profit organization and
sales of AMC books fund our mission of
protecting the Northeast outdoors. If you appreciate our
efforts and would like make a donation to the AMC,
contact us at
Appalachian Mountain Club,
5 Joy Street, Boston, MA 02108.
www.outdoors.org/publications/books/

© Copyright 2008 by Judith Hansen
Illustrations by Donna Sabaka
Book Design by Corinna Dibble
Cover Design by Corinna Dibble
Published by Appalachian Mountain Club Books, 5 Joy Street,
    Boston, MA 02108

Distributed by the Globe Pequot Press, Guilford, Connecticut.

Library of Congress Cataloging-in-Publication Data
Hansen, Judith, 1944-
    Seashells in my pocket : AMC's family guide to exploring the coast from
Maine to Florida / by Judith Hansen ; illustrated by Donna Sabaka. -- 3rd ed.
    p. cm.
    ISBN 978-1-929173-61-7
    1. Seashore animals--Atlantic Coast (U.S.)--Identification--Juvenile
literature. 2. Seashore plants--Atlantic Coast (U.S.)--Identification--Juvenile
literature. 3. Shells--Atlantic Coast (U.S.)--Identification--Juvenile literature.
I. Sabaka, Donna R., ill. II. Title.
QH104.5.A84H36 2008
578.769'90974--dc22
                        2007037315

The paper used in this publication meets the minimum requirements of the
American National Standard for Information Sciences—Permanence of pa-
per for Printed Library Materials, ANSI Z39.48-1984.
Printed on recycled paper.
Printed in the United States of America.

10 9 8 7 6 5 4 3 2 1

CONTENTS

Seashells in My Pocket

is dedicated to our children,
Amy, Jason, and Justin; to our grandchildren,
Savannah, Rachel, Carly, Rebecca,
Sophie, and MacKenzie;
and to young sea-searchers everywhere.

PREFACE

Seashells in My Pocket is written for children ages six and up who enjoy the seashore. While using this guidebook, young adventurers will learn not only the names of many plants and animals, but where and how they live. Older children will be able to use this book by themselves, either as a guide for exploring the coast or as a resource for school projects. Younger children can enjoy this book with the help of an adult or older sibling. Since it was first published in 1988, *Seashells* has been popular with adults as well.

The writing style is straightforward and the language is simple, but some terms that pertain to the seashore might be unfamiliar to young readers. Words that appear in italics can be found in the Glossary.

Children enjoy a challenge, but they thrive on achievement. The authors have been careful to include only those species that are common along the Atlantic Coast so that young readers can realistically complete the checklist at the back of the book. When they have identified all of the plants and animals on the list, they can fill in the Sea-Searcher's Award.

The text and illustrations allow young readers to compare the different species and to distinguish one from the other easily. Rule marks are printed on the back cover to help with field identifications.

Everyone loves pretty seashells, and this book devotes a section to shells that may be collected. The emphasis, however, is on enjoying and identifying coastal plants and animals in their natural habitat, without removing or disturbing them. We hope that adults who use this book with children or students will reinforce that message.

There is always something new to learn when visiting the seashore. *Seashells in My Pocket* can be an introduction to a lifetime of exploring and learning about nature along the seashore.

1 ✳ EXPLORING THE SEASHORE

Thousands of plants and animals live on the coast and in the sea. The plants and animals described in this book are easy to find along the Atlantic Coast from Maine to Florida. Some of them can be seen inland, away from the coast, and in other places in North America. A few may be found in or near other oceans. The map that appears with each *species* shows where, along the Atlantic Coast, the plant or animal is commonly found. Just as some plants and animals can live only in fresh water, others must live in seawater. For example, if you took a trout from a lake and put it in the ocean, the trout would die. If you took a crab from the ocean and put it in a lake, the crab would die. This is not true of all animals and plants, but it is true for most things that live in water.

It is also true that different plants and animals live in different oceans of the world and even in different parts, or *ecosystems,* of the same ocean. An ecosystem includes plants and animals as well as nonliving things, such as rocks and sand. Within each ecosystem are *habitats* that are suitable for different plants and animals. For instance, some ocean life needs deep, cold water; some needs shallow, warm water. Some living things make their homes in the rocks, others in the sand, mud, or dune grass.

If you live near the ocean or have ever visited the ocean, you might have noticed that it seems to be moving all the time. And it is. Twice each day, the water slowly moves up the shore and then slowly moves back out. When the seawater has reached its highest point on the land, it is called *high tide.* Seawater at its lowest point is called *low tide.*

Tides are caused by the pull of the moon's gravity on the Earth. At high tide, the land is facing the moon, which pulls the seawater toward shore; at low tide, the ocean faces the moon, and it pulls the water away from the shore.

The best time to explore the coast is during low tide. The ocean leaves shells, seaweed, and other treasures behind as it goes out. Many shorebirds come to feed on the small plants and animals. *Tide pools*, which are pools of water left among the rocks and in low places on the beach when the tide goes out, are full of living plants and animals to watch.

Look for clues to help you identify the plants and animals that you find. You can identify a plant or animal by its color, size, shape, and the place where you find it. You can also identify an animal by its "behavior," which is the way it acts. When making identifications, it helps to compare the animals or plants to each other.

The next time you visit the coast, use the list at the back of this book to check off each plant, animal, and shell that you see. If you find everything on the list, you will earn the Sea-Searcher's Award. Fill in your name, and hang the award on your wall or put it in a scrapbook.

Exploring the coast and beachcombing are fun all year long. Coastal plants are beautiful even without their flowers. One of the best times to find plant and animal treasures from the sea is after a winter storm. You can see different kinds of shorebirds by visiting the same place on the coast at different times of the year. Many birds *migrate* as the seasons change, flying to a warmer *climate* further south on the coast during the winter, and to a cooler place, further north, for the summer. During migration seasons—spring and fall—you might see an unusual bird species visiting your backyard as the bird travels from its winter home to its summer home.

Most explorers need some equipment and special clothing. They also have rules to protect themselves, the places they explore, and the wildlife they study.

WHAT TO WEAR

1. Sneakers (not your best ones!) or other rubber-soled shoes. They will protect your feet and keep you from slipping on the rocks.
2. A jacket or shirt with pockets, for carrying shells that might break easily.
3. On sunny days, sunglasses or a hat with a visor to protect your eyes.
4. If you're exploring in wooded or grassy areas, wear a long-sleeved shirt and long pants, tucked into your socks, to protect yourself from ticks or other biting insects.

TEN THINGS TO TAKE

1. A friend. It's safer—and more fun—to go exploring with a buddy or an adult.
2. Insect spray and sunscreen lotion.
3. A plastic bag for collecting samples of plants and shells. Remember, take only one sample of each and don't collect living animals or whole living plants.
4. A pencil and a drawing pad if you like to draw pictures.
5. A magnifying glass for taking a closer look at tiny plants and creatures.
6. Binoculars for a closer view of wildlife.
7. A pair of scissors (with safe, rounded tips) for cutting small pieces of seaweed or live plants.
8. A pair of gloves—rubber, latex, or even lightweight gardening gloves will do. You can use them to pick up prickly things or an animal with a sharp-edged shell. They also might come in handy when you're looking for things in the sand or in tide pools.
9. This guidebook.
10. A backpack in which to carry everything, so your hands will be free to pick up samples and to climb safely on the rocks.

A FEW SAFETY RULES

1. Slippery rocks. Rocks that are covered with seaweed are very slippery. Even rocks that look bare are often covered with tiny plants called *algae* that are also very slippery. Your rubber-soled shoes will help, but be careful where you step.
2. Dangerous ocean *currents*. In some places along the coast there are strong currents, such as *undertow*, that can pull you quickly out into deep water. If you are exploring a part of the coast where you have never been

4

before, you or a grown-up can check with a lifeguard or a police officer to find out if there is anything special you should know about the area.

3. *Surf.* Never walk out onto rocks where the surf is crashing. Big waves are beautiful and exciting, but they can knock a person over in a flash.

4. The tides. Sometimes sandy or rocky points that you can walk to at low tide become islands, or are completely under water, when the tide comes back in. Such places are fun to explore, but you don't want to get stranded. Before you begin your seashore adventure, find out when the tide is going out and coming in. In cities and towns along the coast, you can get a chart that shows when the tide will be low and when it will be high. The local newspaper usually prints a *tide chart*, and you often can find one at a supermarket, library, or at the police station. The times for high tide and low tide change slightly each day, so if you're visiting the shore for several days or more, be sure to check the tides every day.

Some Rules to Protect the Environment

1. Never collect live animals or whole living plants. You will find many empty shells, shells with dead animals in them, and pieces of seaweed tossed up on the beach and rocks that you can collect. If you need a sample of a living plant or of a large clump of seaweed, use your scissors to snip off a small piece.

2. When collecting shells, take only one of each type. Even the dead plants and animals are an important part of seashore life. They become food and shelter for living animals. The Hermit Crab, for instance, lives in an empty snail shell. You will learn more about Hermit Crabs in Chapter 2.

5

3. When exploring sand *dunes*, walk only on marked paths. Dune grass, which is very *fragile*, helps keep the sand from blowing away. Also, some birds make their nests there.

4. When picking up a live animal for a closer look, handle it gently. There are special hints about handling live animals in the chapters that follow.

5. In addition to the treasures of the coast, you will find trash that people have tossed from boats or left at the beach. You can help keep the seashore clean if you pick up trash left by others. Some beachcombers take along an extra plastic bag for taking away trash that they find. Then they throw it in a trash bin on the beach or take it home with them to throw away. If you take a snack along, make sure you don't leave any trash behind.

2 ✳ SEA CREATURES

In this chapter, you will find out about living animals that you can see on the Atlantic Coast. The size given for each animal is that of an adult. Many of the animals you see will not be full grown, so they might be smaller than the sizes listed in this book. But you can use the descriptions and illustrations to identify them.

STARFISH

It is easy to identify starfish, or sea stars, as they are sometimes called. They look like stars. A starfish is not a fish, though. It does not have *gills* or *fins*. And it does not have a skeleton. Its underside is soft, and the top of its body has a tough covering that feels like leather.

Starfish live on the bottom of the ocean in both deep and shallow water. Sometimes dead starfish wash up on the beach, but you can often see living starfish in tide pools. On the southern coast they live along sandy shores and in coral *reefs*.

If you see a starfish in the water, it may not be moving or even look alive, but if you pick it up and turn it over (handle the starfish gently), it will probably wave some of its tiny feet at you. Underneath each arm are hundreds of little suction-cup feet that the starfish uses to move along the rocks or sand and to hold its food.

At the end of each arm you will see an orange spot, called an *eyespot*. A starfish can't see, but it can sense light and dark with its eyespots. In the center of the starfish, you will see a small circle. That is the starfish's mouth, which it uses in a very unusual way. To eat its favorite foods (mussels and clams) the starfish wraps its arms around the animal's shell and pulls it open a little bit. Then the starfish pushes its stomach out of its body through its mouth and into the open shell. It digests the animal, then slides its stomach out of the empty shell and back inside its own body.

After you have finished looking at the starfish, put it back in the water. A starfish can live out of the water for only a few minutes. Most starfish included in this book have five arms. The Slender Sea Star might have six arms. The Smooth Sun Star, which looks like a sunflower, can have from seven to fourteen arms. Sometimes you might see a starfish with one or two arms missing because of a fight or an accident, but don't worry. This animal can grow (*regenerate*) a new one. The colors listed for each type of starfish describe the animal's color on top.

BLOOD STAR

COLOR: *red, pink, purple, orange, yellow, or white*
SIZE: *8 inches across*

CUSHION STAR

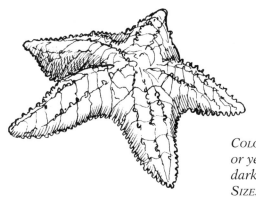

COLOR: *adults are red, orange, or yellow; young are green or dark purple*
SIZE: *10 inches across (from the tip of one point to the tip of the opposite point)*

The largest sea star on the Atlantic Coast is the **Cushion Star**. Its fat body is covered on top with a pattern of ridges that looks like a net. Try counting all the rectangles and triangles!

FORBES COMMON SEA STAR

COLOR: tan, brown, or olive green
SIZE: 10 inches across

NORTHERN SEA STAR

COLOR: orange, pink, gray, tan, lavender, or blue
SIZE: 16 inches across

The **Slender Sea Star** has long, narrow arms. The **Northern Sea Star** has a soft, fat body; on top of each arm, there is a thin row of tiny spines that looks like a white line. The Slender, Northern and **Forbes Common** sea stars are bumpy on top, while the **Blood Star** and the **Smooth Sun Star** are smooth.

SLENDER SEA STAR

COLOR: red, pink, lavender, or purple
SIZE: 3 inches across

SMOOTH SUN STAR

COLOR: purple, red, pink, or orange
SIZE: 16 inches across

THORNY SEA STAR

COLOR: purple, red, or orange
SIZE: 8 inches across

Look for the **Thorny Sea Star** on sunny days, because it is attracted to light. Its small body is covered with rows of large spines.

SEA URCHIN

A living sea urchin is covered with long spines that it uses in two ways. Bits of seaweed that stick to the spines disguise it from enemies. The sea urchin also uses the spines on its underside to move along the sand or rocks. You can find live sea urchins in tide pools and on rocks or sand in shallow water.

The spines won't hurt you, so you can pick up sea urchins for a closer look. Careful, though! Like starfish, this creature has many tiny feet that could be hurt if you pick them up roughly. Sea urchins use their feet to gather food as well as to cling to rocks. Also like the starfish, the sea urchin's mouth is on the underside of its body, in the center.

Sea urchins like to hide, so you might have to turn over a rock or lift a clump of seaweed to find one. If you move

ATLANTIC PURPLE SEA URCHIN

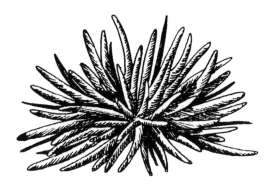

COLOR: purple-brown
SIZE: 2 inches across,
³/₄ inch high

GREEN SEA URCHIN

COLOR: green
SIZE: 3 ¹/₄ inches across,
1 ¹/₂ inches high

a rock, do it slowly and carefully so you won't crush sea urchins and other animals that might be hiding underneath. The shells of dead sea urchins are very pretty and easy to find on many beaches. Look for the illustration of an empty sea urchin shell in Chapter 3.

Sand Dollar

Sand dollars are beautiful animals. They are flat and round like a cookie, with a five-point star design on top. Living sand dollars are covered with short spines. If you pick up a sand dollar and turn it over, you will see a small hole in the center. That is its mouth. Sand dollars can be found in tide pools, on the beach, or in Turtle Grass (see Chapter 6).

Common Sand Dollar

Color: *light brown*
Size: *3 inches across*

The **Common Sand Dollar** has a fancy design on top. All the lines and shapes in the design are in groups of five. Look for ten rows (five pairs) of ovals shaped like kernels of corn. There are five "kernels" in each row. Between each pair of kernel rows is a pair of triangles.

14

Keyhole Urchin

Color: tan or gray
Size: 5 ¹/₂ inches across

The **Keyhole Urchin** is a kind of sand dollar. It is larger and not as perfectly round as the Common Sand Dollar. Young Keyhole Urchins have five long, narrow slots in their bodies. Each slot is shaped like the keyhole of a door, which is how this animal got its name. The slots gradually fill in as the animal grows. The **Six-holed Keyhole Urchin** can bury itself in the sand in just a few minutes by turning its body from side to side.

Six-holed Keyhole Urchin

Color: gray, tan, or light brown
Size: 4 ¹/₂ inches across

15

AMERICAN LOBSTER

Early in the nineteenth century, so many lobsters lived off the coast of New England that people could catch enough for a meal in a few minutes using a net or, if they were careful, their bare hands. Today, lobsters are still a popular food, but after many years of lobster fishing, they are much harder to find. Traps are used to catch them. The **American Lobster** lives both in the shallow, calm waters of *coves* and *inlets* and in deep water far out in the ocean.

The lobster has a hard shell on the outside and no skeleton on the inside. As it grows, it sheds its old shell after a new one has grown underneath. This is called *molting*. With their dark green coloring, lobsters can hide easily among rocks or seaweed. (Once in a while people find lobsters that are blue, yellow-green, or even white.)

Lobsters have a trick to help them escape from danger. If a lobster gets a claw caught in the crack of a rock or if another animal grabs the lobster's claw, the lobster can

AMERICAN LOBSTER

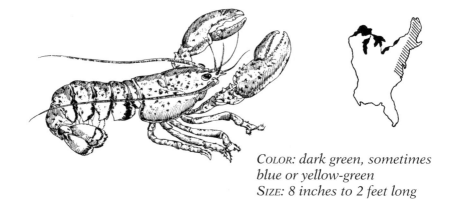

COLOR: *dark green, sometimes blue or yellow-green*
SIZE: *8 inches to 2 feet long*

release the claw from its body and escape. This is called "throwing a claw." Then the lobster grows a new claw in its place. It can also regenerate a new leg or *antenna* if one breaks off or is bitten off.

You probably won't see a live lobster among the rocks. (If you do, don't try to catch it. A lobster's claw is strong enough to break your finger, and the edges of its tail are very sharp.) Along the shore, you are more likely to find pieces of lobster shell, left after a gull's meal or an out-door lobster bake. The dark green shell will have turned red from baking in the sun or over a fire.

CRAB

Many different types of crabs live along the Atlantic Coast. When you're looking for animals in the rocks and seaweed, you will almost certainly find a crab. But you will have to look closely. Like some other animals in the sea and on land, the crab can be hard to see because its coloring helps it blend in with its surroundings. This coloring, which is called *camouflage*, helps to protect the animal from its enemies.

Crabs move sideways, using the claws and feet on one side of their body to push and those on the other side to pull. Crabs move very fast when they sense danger, so you might not see one close up unless it's dead. If you're quick enough to catch a crab, hold it from the back as you would a turtle, so that it can't pinch you with its claws, or *pincers*. A small crab can't harm you, but even a little pinch from a tiny claw could startle you. Dropping the crab might hurt or even kill the animal.

Most adult crabs, and their close relatives, lobsters and shrimp, have eyes that are very different from other animals. A crab's eyes are on top of a flexible body part called an *eyestalk*, which sticks up from its head. Some eyestalks are short and some are quite long, depending on the type of crab. These eyestalks work somewhat like a periscope on a submarine. If a crab wants to come out of the sand or out from under a rock, it sticks its eyestalks up high to make sure it's safe before venturing out. A crab can move its eyestalks back, forth, and around, and even bend them down flat against its shell. If a crab is digging its way into the sand, it flattens its eyestalks so they won't be damaged.

Many scientists believe that a crab's eyes can see light, shadows, and moving shapes, but not sharp details of its surroundings. No one knows if a crab can see different colors. The length and color of the eyestalks can help to identify a crab, but the easiest way is to check the color on the top of the crab's shell.

Acadian Hermit Crab

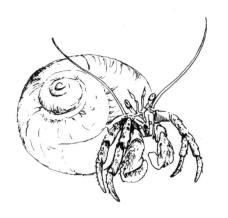

Color: brown
Size: 1 ¼ inches long, 1 inch wide

The **Acadian Hermit Crab** is larger than the Long-Clawed Hermit Crab. It sometimes lives in a Moon Snail shell. Its pincers are also its front walking legs, and the right pincer-leg is much larger than the left. Its legs are orange or brownish red, with an orange stripe on the pincers. It has blue antennae and yellow eyes.

ARROW CRAB

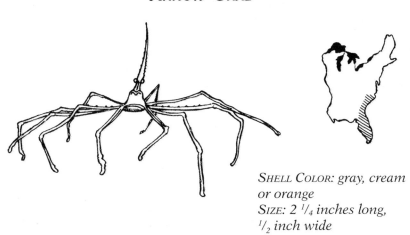

SHELL COLOR: gray, cream or orange
SIZE: 2 $\frac{1}{4}$ inches long, $\frac{1}{2}$ inch wide

With its small body and long, spindly legs, the **Arrow Crab** looks more like its relative, the spider. It is a small crab but easy to identify and, on some parts of the Florida coast, you can see dozens of them picking their way daintily along the Turtle Grass beds. They also can be found on rocks and wharf pilings. Named for its arrow-shaped head and V-shaped stripes, the Arrow Crab is a colorful animal with red legs, brighter red joints, and blue pincers. They have bulging, dark-red eyes on short eyestalks.

ATLANTIC MOLE CRAB

SHELL COLOR: light gray or tan
SIZE: 1 inch long, $^3/_4$ inch wide

The best way to find an **Atlantic Mole Crab** is with your toes. They burrow in the wet sand and you can feel them when you walk along the edge of the water. You can also find them by digging in the wet sand. They can't hurt you because they don't have big claws as other crabs do. Their eyestalks are quite short. The Atlantic Mole Crab has a smooth body, shaped like a little barrel.

ATLANTIC ROCK CRAB

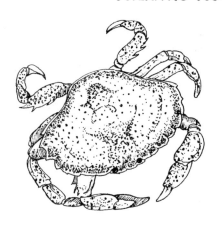

SHELL COLOR: yellow with many red spots
SIZE: 5 $^1/_4$ inches wide, 3 $^1/_2$ inches long

20

The **Atlantic Rock Crab** has red spots, and its legs and short, fat pincers are bright orange. The Atlantic Rock Crab lives along the *low-tide line*. This crab is a popular seafood.

BLUE CRAB

SHELL COLOR: *blue-green or gray-blue*
SIZE: *9 $\frac{1}{4}$ inches wide, 4 inches long*

The **Blue Crab** has large, strong pincers and there are sharp points along the front edge of its body, so if you pick up a Blue Crab, handle it carefully. The male has bright blue markings on its legs and pincers; the female has red markings. Its back legs are shaped like paddles, which help this crab to be a fast swimmer. The Blue Crab is a popular seafood. You can see this crab near the low-tide line. The Blue Crab is especially common in Chesapeake Bay in Maryland.

COMMON SPIDER CRAB

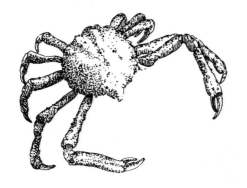

SHELL COLOR: *gray or brown*
SIZE: *3 ³/₄ inches wide,*
4 inches long

The **Common Spider Crab** is easy to identify. All crabs have eight legs but the Spider Crab is the only crab that looks just like a big, fat spider. It lives along the low-tide line.

GHOST CRAB

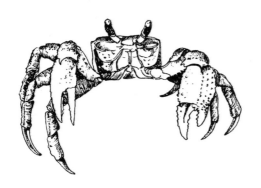

SHELL COLOR: *light gray or*
yellow-white
SIZE: *2 inches wide,*
1 ³/₄ inches long

The **Ghost Crab** makes its home in the sand right on the beach. The name tells about the way this crab acts and looks. Ghost Crabs are yellowish white—just the color of the sand in which they live—with white pincers. They run very fast, on their tiptoes, and they go in and out of the sand so quickly that they seem to disappear and reappear like magic. Their black eyes on the end of their long eye-stalks stick up high above their bodies.

GREEN CRAB

SHELL COLOR: green with black markings
SIZE: 3 inches wide, 2 ¹/₂ inches long

Tide pools are good places to look for **Green Crabs**. They are green and black on top and have large pincers that are both the same size. Green Crabs are especially common on the Maine coast.

JONAH CRAB

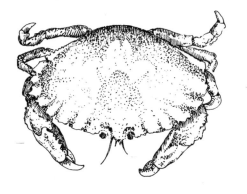

SHELL COLOR: brick red
SIZE: 6 $\frac{1}{4}$ inches wide,
4 inches long

The **Jonah Crab** is about the same size as the Atlantic Rock Crab, and its claws look the same. But the Jonah Crab shell is oval and is the color of red brick. This crab lives in rocks and seaweed.

LADY CRAB

SHELL COLOR: gray or tan with dark purple spots
SIZE: 3 inches wide,
2 $\frac{1}{2}$ inches long

The **Lady Crab** looks like it has the measles; its shell is covered with spots. Wait for low tide and look for this crab along the water's edge. *But don't try to pick up a Lady Crab.* They are not shy like most crabs, and they have long pincers that are very sharp.

LONG-CLAWED HERMIT CRAB

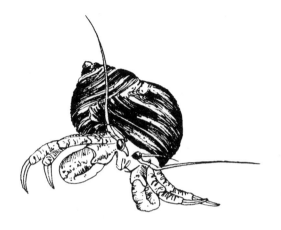

BODY COLOR: gray or green-white
SIZE: $^1/_2$ inch long, $^3/_8$ inch wide

The **Long-Clawed Hermit Crab** is the most common type of hermit crab on the Atlantic Coast. This crab is so small that it can live in a periwinkle shell. The Long-Clawed Hermit Crab has tan pincers; some have a tan stripe on each pincer.

When you're looking for a hermit crab, don't look for a crab. Look for a snail shell. That's where a hermit crab lives. Unlike other crabs, a hermit crab has no shell of its own. It must use the empty shell of another animal for protection. If you see a snail shell moving fast instead of slowly, you can be sure there's a hermit crab inside.

Hermit crabs often can be found in tide pools and sometimes on the beach. When left on the beach by the tide, some sea animals dry out and die or are eaten by other animals. But the hermit crab just pulls far back into its shell and waits for the next high tide.

Like most other crabs, the hermit crab has two claws that it uses to catch its food and to protect itself. A hermit crab's right claw is always larger than its left. It uses its

25

claws to pull its borrowed home along the rocks and sand. As the crab grows, it looks for a larger shell. Before moving in, the hermit crab pokes its claw inside the new shell to make sure the shell is empty.

A hermit crab often shares its home with a small worm. The two animals help each other. The crab protects the worm, and the worm keeps the inside of the shell clean by eating small bits of garbage.

SAND FIDDLER CRAB

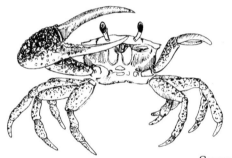

SHELL COLOR: *purple or gray-blue with darker markings; purple patch on top near front*
SIZE: *1 ¹/₂ inches wide, 1 inch long*

You need a good imagination to see how the fiddler crab got its name. Fiddler crabs have one pincer that is much larger than the other. The large pincer looks a little bit like a person's arm when it's playing a fiddle—bent at the elbow and holding a bow. The large pincer is covered with light-colored spots. It has very long eyestalks. The **Sand Fiddler Crab** is a kind of fiddler crab that lives in sandy areas.

STONE CRAB

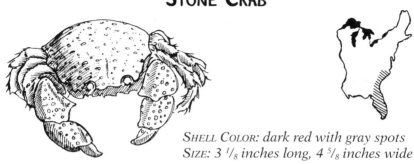

SHELL COLOR: *dark red with gray spots*
SIZE: *3 $\frac{1}{8}$ inches long, 4 $\frac{5}{8}$ inches wide*

The **Stone Crab** is also a popular seafood. It has larger pincers than any other crab on the Atlantic Coast, and it has fat, hairy walking legs. Unlike most crabs, it does not have eyestalks; its eyes are under the top, front edge of its shell. You can find adults in the sand or mud near the low-tide line. Young Stone Crabs often live in Turtle Grass beds.

WHARF CRAB

SHELL COLOR: *dark green or brown*
SIZE: *$\frac{3}{4}$ inch long, $\frac{7}{8}$ inch wide*

Wharf Crabs are small but they are commonly seen because they are so friendly. They live among rocks, near docks and wharfs, and often climb into boats. If a Wharf Crab comes to visit you on a boat, it might be tempting to keep it for a pet. But, like all wild creatures, this little crab will be happier if you return it to its own environment, after exchanging a friendly "hello," of course.

HORSESHOE CRAB

The **Horseshoe Crab** has lived on Earth for more than 350 million years. It is one of the oldest animals creatures on the planet. The Horseshoe Crab lived with dinosaurs and looks the same today as it did then. One reason it has survived for so long is that it can live in very cold or very hot water. It can even survive being frozen in ice. The Horseshoe Crab is related to other crabs, but it is not really a crab. The Horseshoe Crab has body parts more like those of its closer relatives, the spider and the scorpion.

The Horseshoe Crab has a smooth, brown shell that is shaped like a horse's hoof. Along the bottom edge of the shell is a hard, horseshoe-shaped rim that it uses like a shovel to burrow into the sand or mud to find worms and clams to eat.

A Horseshoe Crab has nine eyes—seven on top of its shell and two underneath—and several light sensors, but it cannot see very well. It's not a very good swimmer, either.

It has a long, thin, strong tail that helps push the animal forward when it burrows. The tail also comes in handy when the Horseshoe Crab gets turned upside down on the ocean floor. It uses its tail to flip itself over. When you find a Horseshoe Crab, turn it gently over on its back. It is surprising how quickly the animal can flip itself over. Sometimes Horseshoe Crabs get washed up on the beach by waves and get stranded upside down on the beach as the tide goes out. If they are upside down on land, they can't turn themselves over and could die before the next high tide. If you see a Horseshoe Crab upside down on the beach, gently turn it over by pushing on one side of its shell. Don't pick it up by its tail because it could be damaged or even break off. It has small claws on its pincers (used for eating) and on six of its eight legs, but the claws won't hurt you.

HORSESHOE CRAB

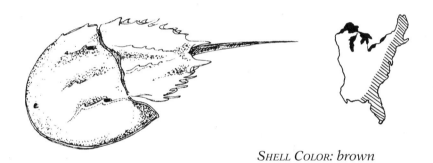

SHELL COLOR: brown
SIZE: 2 feet long, 1 foot wide

"Appendix A: Sea-Searching on the Internet," includes a Web site where you can learn more about the amazing Horseshoe Crab.

A Horseshoe Crab has four eyes on top of its shell, and several light sensors underneath, but it cannot see very well. (It's not a very good swimmer, either.)

BEACH FLEA

If you have ever been to an ocean beach, you probably have seen this annoying little creature. The beach flea is much larger than the flea you might find on your dog, but fortunately, it does not bite dogs or people. A beach flea is not an insect; it is related to crabs, shrimp, and lobster. Like many insects, however, the beach flea is a great jumper, which is why it is sometimes called a sand hopper. Beach fleas can swim, but they are most often seen in great numbers on piles of seaweed and other trash on the beach.

The **Big-Eyed Beach Flea** is the most common beach flea on the Atlantic Coast. As you might guess, it has very large eyes.

BIG-EYED BEACH FLEA

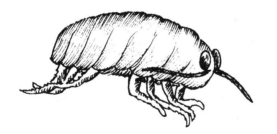

COLOR: *dark brown or gray*
SIZE: *³/₄ inch long*

BARNACLE

This animal spends its whole adult life standing on its head. A barnacle begins life as a tiny worm called a *larva*. The larva floats in the water until it grows into an adult barnacle. Then it cements itself, head down, onto a rock, wharf, shell, or boat bottom. (The cement is limestone, which the barnacle makes from seawater.) The barnacle stays there for the rest of its life.

The barnacle eats by opening a tiny hole like a trapdoor at the top of its shell. It sticks out its tiny, feathery feet and kicks food into its mouth. You can watch a barnacle eat if you find one that is underwater. When the tide goes out, the barnacle closes the hole tightly to protect itself from the hot sun. Barnacles live together in large groups, called *colonies*.

BAY BARNACLE

SHELL COLOR: *shiny white*
SIZE: *¹/₄ inch high, ¹/₂ inch wide*

IVORY BARNACLE

COLOR: creamy white
SIZE: 1 inch high, 1 inch wide

LARGE ROCK BARNACLE

COLOR: gray-white
SIZE: $^3/_4$ inch high,
1 $^1/_4$ inches wide

LITTLE GRAY BARNACLE

COLOR: gray-white
SIZE: $^1/_4$ inch high,
$^1/_8$ inch wide

NORTHERN ROCK BARNACLE

COLOR: white
SIZE: 1 inch high,
¹/₂ inch wide

LIMPET

The limpet is a small, cone-shaped animal that looks like a little hat. Some types of limpets have a small hole in the top of the cone. Its shell may be smooth or rough. Most limpets have brown and white stripes that run from the bottom of their shells to the top. A limpet makes its home by rubbing a shallow hole into a rock with its hard shell. The limpet can hold on to the rock so tightly that it can't be moved even by strong ocean waves. The limpet sometimes leaves its home at high tide, but it returns at low tide to eat.

The **Atlantic Plate Limpet** has a smooth shell and is sometimes called the "tortoise shell" limpet because of the pattern of its brown markings. The **Cayenne Keyhole Limpet** has a small hole at the top. It is not quite as rounded as the Atlantic Plate Limpet, and its shell has deep ridges that spread like rays from the top to the outer edge.

ATLANTIC PLATE LIMPET

COLOR: white or tan with dark brown markings
SIZE: $^7/_8$ to 1 $^3/_4$ inches long

CAYENNE KEYHOLE LIMPET

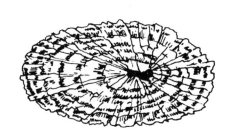

COLOR: dark gray or white with yellowish or light brown markings
SIZE: $^5/_8$ to 1 $^3/_4$ inches long

34

SNAIL

If you watch a snail move, you will see why snails are famous for being slow. A snail has only one foot. If you pick up the snail, you can see its head, with two antennae, and its foot (don't look for toes; the snail's foot is just a muscle). You have to be fast, because when the snail senses danger, it quickly pulls itself inside its shell. You might also try looking at the snail through a magnifying glass while it is moving. You might be able to see the tiny slit that is the snail's mouth. The snail also has a tongue and a row of sharp teeth, which are so small you need a microscope to see them.

Along the beaches and rocky shores of the Atlantic Coast, you will see many different live snails and empty snail shells. You also will see snail trails—lines in the sand left by a snail's single flat foot. In the next chapter, there are more illustrations of snails.

MUSSEL

When you see a mussel at low tide, it's hard to believe it is alive. The two halves of its shell are closed, and it does not move at all. But when the tide comes in, the mussel opens its shell to let in seawater, which is filled with tiny plants and animals that mussels eat. Usually mussels wait for their food to be washed in with the waves, but a mussel can move slowly with its one foot if it needs to find food or protection.

You can find groups of mussels attached to the rocks or lying on the muddy bottoms of coves, *bays*, and saltwater rivers. A mussel attaches itself to rocks (and to other mussels) with strong, thin, brown threads that it produces with a gland in its foot. A group of mussels attached in this way is called a *bed*, or a colony, of mussels. Look for more illustrations of mussels in the next chapter.

A colony of mussels

CHITON

It's hard to tell if this small animal is coming or going. It is a small oval that is shaped a lot like a turtle. If you look at an upside-down chiton, you might be able to see its foot and head, which are close together on one end. The chiton can't move fast, but its foot is very strong. You will find out how strong it is if you try to take a chiton off the rock or shell on which it lives. If you do get it off, it will quickly curl into a ball to protect itself. The **Common Eastern Chiton** is often found on slipper shells. The **Red Northern Chiton** can be found on rocks at low tide.

COMMON EASTERN CHITON

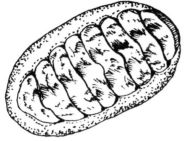

COLOR: *light brown or dirty white*
SIZE: *³/₈ to ³/₄ inch long*

RED NORTHERN CHITON

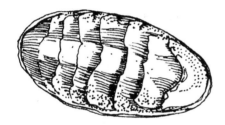

COLOR: *light yellow with red markings*
Size: *¹/₂ to 1 inch long*

JELLYFISH

One good reason to wear shoes while you're exploring the shore is to protect your feet from jellyfish. If you touch a jellyfish, even if it is dead, you will be stung. A jellyfish doesn't sting like a bee. The animal has many tiny stingers that shoot poison "darts" when touched. These darts are so small that you need a microscope to see them. Some jellyfish stings make your skin itch for a few

37

hours. Others can cause painful blisters. Some can kill you. *To be safe, never touch any jellyfish.*

As it floats near the surface of the ocean, a jellyfish uses its darts to kill small sea animals for food. A jellyfish is not really a fish; it has no scales, fins, or gills. It feels and looks like jelly. The jellyfish is made mostly of water, and most of its body is a stomach. It is not a good swimmer, but it can move through the water by opening and closing its body, like an umbrella.

The Moon Jellyfish, the Sea Nettle, and the Lion's Mane Jellyfish—descriptions of which follow—often wash up on Atlantic Coast beaches.

CANNONBALL JELLYFISH

COLOR: *yellow or light blue*
SIZE: *7 inches across*

The **Cannonball Jellyfish**, sometimes called the Jellyball, is named for its round shape. The fat Cannonball Jellyfish has sixteen short *tentacles* that are forked like a slingshot. It floats near the shore from the Chesapeake Bay to Florida.

LION'S MANE JELLYFISH

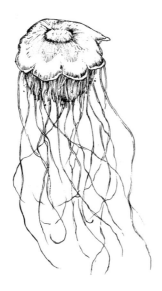

COLOR: changes with age
SIZE: 8 feet across

The **Lion's Mane Jellyfish** is the largest jellyfish in the world. It can grow to be eight feet wide, and it has 150 tentacles. The Lion's Mane Jellyfish changes color as it grows. Young Lion's Mane Jellyfish (up to six inches wide) are pink or yellow; those from six to eighteen inches wide are red or dark yellow; larger ones are dark red or brown. This jellyfish can be found from Canada to Florida. The Lion's Mane Jellyfish is very poisonous. Its sting burns, causes blisters, and can be deadly.

The body of the **Moon Jellyfish** is shaped like a saucer and is mostly white and clear, like water. You can see colored body parts—yellow, brown, and pink—inside. It

MOON JELLYFISH

COLOR: *white and clear*
SIZE: *12 inches across*

has many short tentacles that look like a fringe. On the Atlantic Coast, the Moon Jellyfish often can be seen floating near the shore from Canada to Florida. This jellyfish's sting causes a rash that can itch for several hours.

These creatures are so pretty—bright blue and pink—that it's tempting to touch them, but don't! They are very *toxic*. Their tentacles, which can be as long as 60 feet, are covered with stinging cells that cause severe burns and blisters. They are dangerously poisonous even when they're dead, and sometimes a few of the *venomous* tentacles break off and float away or fall to the ocean floor.

PORTUGUESE MAN-OF-WAR

It's important to stay out of the water if a **Portuguese Man-of-War** is sighted in the area. Children and anyone with allergies or asthma are especially sensitive to the venom.

This unique animal looks like a jellyfish, but it is actually a strange creature made up of four *organisms* called "polyps" that are joined together and live and look like one animal. The part that looks like jelly is an air-filled sack, called a float, that looks and works like a balloon

40

FLOAT COLOR: translucent blue, or violet
CREST COLOR: bright pink, blue, or violet
FLOAT SIZE: 12 inches long, 5 to 6 inches high, and 5 inches wide

that keeps the animal floating on top of the sea. The float is shaped something like a pear.

A Man-of-War, sometimes called a Bluebottle, can't push itself through the water like a jellyfish. The float has a crest several inches high along the top that works like a sail on a boat (in fact, it's named for a type of Portuguese battleship that had a sail); the animal is pushed through the water by the wind and the ocean currents. The float and crest must stay wet for the animal to survive. When a Man-of-War is in the ocean, it rolls to one side from time to time to dip the float and crest into the water. It can also deflate the float and submerge under water for a short time to escape its greatest enemy, the sea turtle, which is immune to the Man-of-War's poison.

Some scientists believe the Portuguese Man-of-War can move its crest or change the shape of its float to shift direction slightly (like a sailor changing the position of a sail to take best advantage of the wind). Others think the animal has no control over where it goes, which could explain why so many are found washed up on the beach, especially on a windy day or after a storm.

The Portuguese Man-of-War can be found in warm ocean waters all over the world. On the East Coast of the United States, they are most commonly seen in Florida, but they have been found as far north as Cape Cod, Massachusetts.

SEA NETTLE

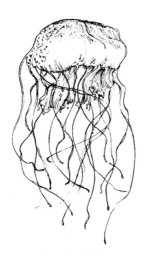

COLOR: pink with red stripes or white
SIZE: 10 inches across (pink) or 4 inches across (white)

There are two different kinds of **Sea Nettle**. One is pink with red stripes; the other is white. The pink Sea Nettle has forty tentacles; the white is smaller and has twenty-four tentacles. Sea Nettles are especially common in Chesapeake Bay, but they can be seen from Cape Cod, Massachusetts, to Florida. The sting of a Sea Nettle causes itching, but a bad sting could cause a more serious reaction.

UPSIDE-DOWN JELLYFISH

COLOR: dark green or muddy yellow
SIZE: 12 inches across

The **Upside-Down Jellyfish** is named for its habit of turning upside down when it sinks to the ocean floor to eat tiny animals that live there. The body of the Upside-Down Jellyfish is shaped like a cookie. Its eight arms, which can be green or brown, look like plants sprouting out of its body. Its sting causes an itchy rash. These jellyfish gather by the hundreds or even the thousands, lying on the bottom of shallow bays along the South coast of Florida.

SEA ANEMONE

A sea anemone looks more like a plant than an animal. Its tentacles look like flower petals as they wave back and forth in the water, catching small sea animals to eat. The sea anemone is closely related to the jellyfish. Like the jellyfish, the sea anemone's tentacles have stingers that help it catch food. (The stingers aren't dangerous to people, but they hurt.) And the sea anemone's body is mostly stomach. But the sea anemone does not float in the water as the jellyfish does. It lives underwater and attaches itself to a rock or sometimes to the hard shell of another animal, such as a crab. Some sea anemones bury themselves in the sand or mud.

Sea anemones can be hard to see because they like to live in dark places, protected from the sunlight. Look closely along the shady side of a tide pool and be very quiet. When the sea anemone senses danger, it pulls its tentacles into its body. Then it looks like a small tree stump or a mushroom. You might be able to watch this happen. When you spot a sea anemone, stay very still for a few minutes. Then make waves in the water with your hand or a stick. The animal will quickly pull in its tentacles.

FRILLED ANEMONE

COLOR: *brown with light-colored tentacles*
SIZE: *18 inches high*

44

GHOST ANEMONE

COLOR: *light yellow and clear*
SIZE: *1 ¹/₂ inches high*

LINED ANEMONE

COLOR: *white or tan*
SIZE: *1 ³/₈ inches high*

STRIPED ANEMONE

COLOR: *brown or green with yellow or orange stripes*
SIZE: *³/₄ inch high*

45

WORM

If you move a large rock near the low-tide line or dig in wet sand, you're likely to see a sea worm wriggling out of sight. Worms that live along the seashore can sting or bite, so if you want to get a closer look, catch the worm in a bucket or put on rubber gloves to protect your hands before you pick one up. You will have to move quickly. Like the night crawlers that might live in your backyard, seashore worms can dig fast. You can also see sea worms in fishing tackle shops because they are used for bait.

CLAM WORM

COLOR: *shiny green or blue on top with tiny red, yellow, or white spots; reddish "paddles" all along its 200 segments*
SIZE: *36 inches long*

LEAFY PADDLE WORM

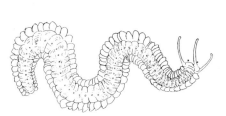 

COLOR: *gray, green, tan, or white*
SIZE: *18 inches long*

46

LIMULUS LEECH

COLOR: *cream or white*
SIZE: *⁵⁄₈ inch long*

This small creature is a good friend of the Horseshoe Crab. It attaches itself to the crab's legs and gills and feeds on tiny pieces of food it finds there. If the **Limulus Leech** is removed from the Horseshoe Crab, it will not eat and it begins to shrink.

TWO-GILLED BLOOD WORM

COLOR: *pale pink*
SIZE: *15 inches long*

47

SPONGE

For many years, experts couldn't decide whether the sponge was a plant or an animal. But finally it was decided that sponges are animals because they "catch" their food by taking water into the tiny holes that cover their bodies. Unlike animals, plants make their own food.

What you see when you look at a sponge is its skeleton. Sponges use the holes that cover them for breathing as well as for collecting food. Some living sponges are covered with sharp little needles, but these are too small to see without a microscope.

Even experts have trouble identifying different sponges because each kind can have many shapes, colors, and sizes. You might see living sponges attached to rocks or shells in tide pools or in shallow, protected places along the shore. You often can find pieces of dead sponges washed up on the beach.

As you can probably guess, the **Crumb-of-Bread Sponge** looks something like a piece of bread—not a slice, but a clump torn from a whole loaf. The **Finger**

CRUMB-OF-BREAD SPONGE

COLOR: tan or light yellow
SIZE: varies, usually found on the beach in clumps that will fit in your hand

Sponge has many long branches that look like fingers. It is tan or pink, but if you find a piece on the beach it might be white, bleached by the sun. The **Red Beard Sponge** has fuzzy, red-orange branches.

FINGER SPONGE

COLOR: tan or pink
SIZE: grows to 18 inches high

RED BEARD SPONGE

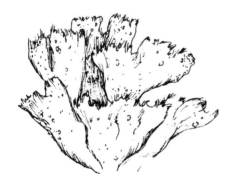

COLOR: red or orange
SIZE: varies from very thin layer to 8 inches thick

49

- What animal has an egg case that looks like a necklace?
- What shells are decorated with letters of the alphabet?
- What animal's skeleton is called "the jewel box of the sea"?

3 ✳ SHELLS TO COLLECT

When you explore the shore, you might see the shells of some of the animals described in Chapter 2. You will also find the shells of other sea creatures washed up on the beach or rocks. All the shells described in this chapter are *mollusks*, except for the sand dollar and the sea urchin.

A mollusk is an animal with a soft body that is protected by a hard shell. Some mollusks have one shell; some have two shells connected by a *hinge*. Many of the shells that you collect will be half of a two-shelled mollusk. But sometimes you can find an empty two-shelled mollusk that is still connected at the hinge.

On the inside of a two-shelled mollusk shell, you can usually see where the animal's foot, or muscle, was attached. Sometimes the spot is a darker color than the rest of the inside of the shell. This spot is called a *muscle scar*. Sometimes the color of the muscle scar can help you identify the shell.

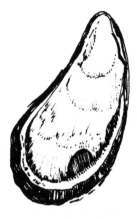

Muscle scar   *Muscle with skin*

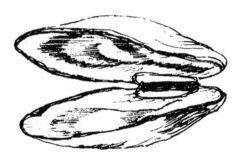

Mollusk with hinge

One-shelled mollusk with growth lines

Two-shelled mollusk with growth lines

You can see how a mollusk has grown by its *growth lines*. On both one- and two-shelled mollusks, these growth lines curve together all around the shell. Sometimes these growth lines are flat, and sometimes they are ridges that you can see and feel easily.

Some mollusk shells, such as mussel or clam shells, are partly covered with a brown or black "skin." This skin protects the shell from dissolving in the seawater. The "skin" is soft when the animal is in the water. It becomes dry and feels like thin paper after the empty shell has been on the rocks or sand for a while.

The size given with each shell description is the average size of a full-grown animal. You will find many shells that are smaller, and perhaps some that are larger, than the sizes shown in this guidebook.

SAND DOLLAR

You can learn about living sand dollars in Chapter 2, "Sea Creatures." Like sea urchins, sand dollars lose their spines after they die. This shell is fragile, so carry it carefully.

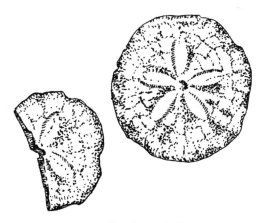

Sand Dollar shells

SEA URCHIN

You also can find out about living sea urchins in Chapter 2, "Sea Creatures." The skeleton of a dead sea urchin is sometimes called the "jewel box of the sea" because of its beauty. You might find a dead sea urchin with all or most of its spines gone. You can see the many perfect rows of bumps where the spines were attached. Like sand dollar shells, sea urchin shells are fragile.

Sea Urchin shells

ATLANTIC DOGWINKLE

This is a common shell, but it is sometimes difficult to identify because its color and shape vary, depending on what it eats and where it lives. Those that eat Blue Mussels have a dark shell—brown or reddish brown. Those that eat barnacles are lighter-colored—white, yellow, or light brown. The thick shell of the **Atlantic Dogwinkle** is covered with ridges. Atlantic Dogwinkles that live where the ocean has big waves have smaller ridges than those that live where the water is calm.

ATLANTIC DOGWINKLE

SIZE: $^7/_8$ inch to 2 inches long

ATLANTIC OYSTER DRILL

SIZE: $^1/_2$ to 1 $^3/_4$ inches long

The **Atlantic Oyster Drill** is named for its favorite food—the oyster—and for the way it eats an oyster. It drills a hole in an oyster's shell and eats the soft body inside. The spiral-shaped shell is gray or brown and covered with thin ridges. You will find the Atlantic Oyster Drill wherever you find oysters. The Atlantic Oyster Drill also eats mussels and barnacles, so you might find one among the rocks or on a beach near rocks.

PERIWINKLE

Periwinkles can live out of water for a longer time than many other sea creatures. The **Common Periwinkle** has a dark-colored shell—gray, brown, or black. It is very common among rocks and seaweed. The **Northern Yellow Periwinkle** is very small. It is light-colored—usually yellow, but sometimes white, orange, or tan. It has a smooth, shiny shell. Look for this periwinkle among rocks. The **Marsh Periwinkle** lives in salt *marshes*, but it is often found on beaches where it has been washed up by the waves. This periwinkle is white with brown spots.

COMMON PERIWINKLE

SIZE: ⁵⁄₈ to 1 ¹⁄₂ inches long

MARSH PERIWINKLE

SIZE: ³⁄₄ to 1 inch long

NORTHERN YELLOW PERIWINKLE

SIZE: $^3/_8$ to $^3/_4$ inch long

WHELK

There are two large whelks that are commonly found on beaches from Cape Cod, Massachusetts, to Florida. They are the **Knobbed Whelk** and the **Channelled Whelk**. It is easy to tell these two whelks apart. The Channelled Whelk has a smooth shell that is tan or grayish on the outside and light pink on the inside. The Knobbed Whelk is tan with brown streaks on the outside and orange on the inside. It has rows of big bumps (knobs) on the fat part of the shell. Both of these whelks are found in sandy places.

CHANNELLED WHELK

SIZE: $3^1/_2$ to $7^1/_2$ inches long

Of all the whelks described in this book, the **Eastern Mud Whelk** is the most common. It is also the smallest. This whelk is known by several different names, but part of its name is always "mud": Common Mud Snail, Mud Dog Whelk, Eastern Mud Nassa, and Mud Basket. You may have guessed that the best place to look for this shell is in, or near, mud. The Eastern Mud Whelk has a thick spiral shell that is usually a dark color—brown, reddish brown, or almost black.

EASTERN MUD WHELK

Size: $\frac{5}{8}$ to 1 $\frac{1}{4}$ inches long

KNOBBED WHELK

Size: 4 to 9 inches long

NEW ENGLAND BASKET WHELK

SIZE: $1/2$ to $7/8$ inch long

The **New England Basket Whelk** is another small whelk with several different names. It is sometimes called the New England Nassa, the New England Dog Whelk, or the Three-Lined Basket Shell. Even though it has "New England" in its name, it is found all along the Atlantic Coast from Canada to Florida. It has a bumpy, spiral-shaped shell that is tan, yellowish-gray, or light orange. The New England Basket Whelk is found in sand or mud.

Whelk egg case

The egg cases of these and other large whelks are fun to find on the beach. They look like necklaces: papery tan disks about the size of a nickel or a quarter connected with a string. Sometimes the disks are filled with hundreds of tiny shells.

JUJUBE TOP SHELL

SIZE: up to 1 inch long

You might think the **Jujube Top Shell** was named after those fruit-flavored little candies with the same name. But the shell and the candy are both named for the fruit of the jujube tree. This shell, like the fruit, is shaped like a short, fat cone. It is light yellow or brown covered with a mottled pattern of white. Several parallel ridges circle the shell from the point of the cone to the bottom.

CHESTNUT TURBAN

SIZE: 1 to ³/₄ inches long

The **Chestnut Turban** shell could be named for the color of a chestnut—brown—or even for its rough surface, which some might think looks like the outside of a chestnut seed. It is shaped like a turban—pointed on one end, rounded, then wide on the other. The outside has many rows of parallel bumpy lines and an uneven pattern of white or light yellow.

60

SHARK EYE

SIZE: $^7/_8$ to 3 inches long

The **Shark Eye** shell is smooth and shiny. It is white on the inside and gray, light brown, or light blue on the outside. On one side of the top is a beautiful swirl that looks like the number six (or the number nine). The middle of the swirl looks like an eye, which is how the shell got its name. Living Shark Eyes eat clams and other sea creatures that live in the sand, so you will probably find this shell on a sandy beach.

COMMON NORTHERN MOON SNAIL

SIZE: 1 $\frac{1}{2}$ to 5 inches long

    The **Common Northern Moon Snail** has an "eye" on one side of its outer shell, just as the Shark Eye does. But it is probably named for the half moon–shaped opening of its shell. The Common Northern Moon Snail has a light gray or light yellow shell with darker-colored streaks. It is brown or tan on the inside. This shell is smooth, but not as shiny as the Shark Eye. The Common Northern Moon Snail can be found in the wet sand at low tide.

COMMON ATLANTIC SLIPPER SHELL

SIZE: $\frac{3}{4}$ to 2 $\frac{1}{2}$ inches long

62

Slipper shells are often found attached to other shells, such as a mussel or a scallop or a Horseshoe Crab. You might also see slipper shells attached to each other in a pile. The top of the **Common Atlantic Slipper Shell** is rounded. It is white with many thin, brown lines. When you look at the inside of the shell, you will see how the slipper shell got its name. A thin "shelf" covers half of the shell, like the top of a slipper covers your foot.

CUP-AND-SAUCER SHELL

SIZE: 1 inch long

The **Cup-and-Saucer Shell**, like the limpet, looks like a pointed hat. The Cup-and-Saucer Shell is larger and more round on the bottom than the limpet. Living Cup-and-Saucers attach themselves to rocks, just as limpets do. But the easiest way to identify the Cup-and-Saucer Shell is by the small "cup" that is attached to the inside of the "saucer." The outside of the saucer is white or tan. The inside is brown and the cup is white.

COMMON JINGLE SHELL

SIZE: ³/₄ to 2 ¹/₄ inches long

The **Common Jingle Shell** is named for the sound that is made when several jingle shells are strung together to make a wind chime. Although these shells are so thin you can see through them, they are not too fragile. They feel and even look a little like a wrinkled toenail. This shell is almost flat (except for its wrinkles) and is white, gray, or yellowish. Look for this shell on the beach.

BLEEDING TOOTH

SIZE: 1 to 1 ¹/₂ inches long

If you look inside the **Bleeding Tooth,** you can see how it got its name. There are several little white "teeth" sur-rounded by a red patch. The outside of its shell is dirty white with black and red marks. You can find them on the rocks of tide pools.

64

COMMON DOVE SHELL

SIZE: $^3/_8$ to $^7/_8$ inch long

Shell collectors and people who make jewelry with shells like the **Common Dove Shell** because of its colors and markings. It can be white with orange or yellow spots and lines or it can be brown with white markings. The shell is thick with many ridges on the outside. Look for a row of twelve white "teeth" along the lip.

FLORIDA ROCK SHELL

SIZE: 1 inch long

You can find the animal that lives in the **Florida Rock Shell** alive among the rocks at low tide. It is sometimes called a Florida Dye Shell because it can release colored liquid to hide from its enemies. The short, fat shell is gray with brown spots. It has four or five *whorls*.

SCOTCH BONNET

SIZE: 3 to 4 inches long

Scotch Bonnet is easy to identify. It is pale yellow or white with light-brown squares in an even pattern. This shell can be smooth or have ridges on the outside. It is a thick shell with teeth along the lip. Look for these shells in shallow water or along the beach.

COMMON PURPLE SNAIL

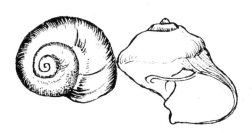

SIZE: 1 to 1 ¹/₂ inches wide

The **Common Purple Snail** is a beautiful shell that seems to glow with shades of light and dark purple. It is a thin and delicate shell so it is difficult to find a whole, perfect one. The best time to look for the Common Purple Snail is after storms in the spring.

66

APPLE MUREX

SIZE: ¹/₂ inch long

Look for the **Apple Murex** in shallow water. It doesn't feel or look like an apple. It is rough with deep ridges all around. The outside is yellowish white with dark-brown markings. Brown marks just inside the shell, near the lip, help identify the Apple Murex.

COMMON AMERICAN SUNDIAL

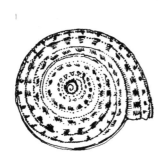

SIZE: 1 to 2 ¹/₂ inches across

You can't tell time with the **Common American Sundial**, but it will be a treasure in your shell collection. The top of the shell has a pattern of swirls and marks that make it look like a pinwheel. The bottom of the shell is flat. It is white or gray with brown or purple markings.

WEST INDIAN WORM SHELL

SIZE: 1 to 5 inches long

With its long body and cone-shaped end, the **West Indian Worm Shell** looks like a worm wearing a party hat. Young worm shells are tightly coiled, but older ones might have only two or three twists. They can be brown or pale yellow. Worm shells are often found near colonies of sponges.

ANGULATE WENTLETRAP

SIZE: 1 inch long

There are many types of wentletraps, but you can tell them apart if you examine them closely. They are sometimes called *staircase shells* because they look like a winding staircase. In fact, the name comes from the Dutch word *wentletrap*, which means "winding staircase." The **Angulate Wentletrap** is shiny white with six or more whorls. Each whorl has nine or ten *ribs*. They are easy to find in the sand.

68

COMMON AMERICAN AUGER

SIZE: 1 $\frac{1}{2}$ to 2 inches long

An auger is the name of a tool that carpenters use to drill holes. And that's what the **Common American Auger** looks like: a small drill. It is sometimes called the Little Screw Shell or the Atlantic Auger. The shell is light or dark gray, with darker bands of brown or dark purple. It has many whorls with twenty to twenty-five ribs on each whorl.

ALPHABET CONE

SIZE: 2 to 3 inches long

You might not find all the letters of the alphabet on the **Alphabet Cone**, but you can see some of them if you use your imagination. The shell is smooth and creamy white with rows of brown and orange markings. It is shaped like a cone with a pointy top.

69

LETTERED OLIVE

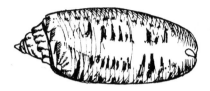

SIZE: 2 $^1/_2$ inches long

The **Lettered Olive** is smooth and oval, like an olive, but longer, with markings that look like the letters V or A. It is a slender shell with several "wrinkles" and creases. This shell can be greenish gray or tan with dark-brown markings.

TRUE TULIP

SIZE: 4 inches long

The **True Tulip** doesn't look at all like a tulip, but the sack that it makes for its eggs does. You might find the flower-like sack in shallow water in the mud or weeds. The shell of the True Tulip has many colors, but it is mostly white with brown marks. The inside is the color of cocoa.

CONCH

Conches are the shells that people like to put up to their ear and say they can hear the ocean roaring. **Florida Crown Conches** are usually found in coastal areas that are shaded by mango trees. There are many types of crown conches with different sizes, shapes, and colors. Many of them have single rows of spines that stand straight up. The best way to identify a Florida Crown Conch is by the seven whorls at the top of the shell (sometimes called the *spire*). The shell is striped with shades of gray, brown, and pale yellow.

FLORIDA CROWN CONCH

SIZE: 3 to 5 inches long

PINK CONCH

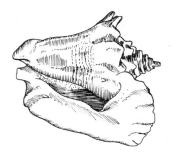

SIZE: 10 inches long

The **Pink Conch** is sometimes called the Queen Conch. It is large and heavy and the inside of the lip is rosy pink. The outside is light yellow or brown. You can identify this shell by its size. Also, look for the side of the shell that sticks out like an open door.

COQUINA

SIZE: $1/2$ to $3/4$ inch long

Coquina are two-shelled mollusks that come in many colors—yellow, pink, purple, blue, red, or white, with patterns of darker colors like rays of sunshine. They look like jewels, and in some places on the coast of Florida there are so many that it looks as if someone dumped out a treasure chest. They are sometimes called butterfly shells because when the two sides of a Coquina shell are hinged together and the open shell is lying flat, the shape looks something like a butterfly.

BUTTERCUP LUCINE

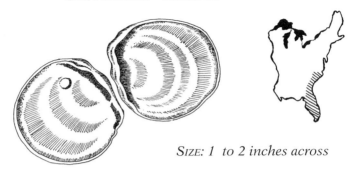

SIZE: 1 to 2 inches across

Almost round and quite fragile, the **Buttercup Lucine** is a pretty shell that is bright yellow or pale orange on the inside. The outside is grayish-white and covered with fine *concentric* growth lines.

CROSS-BARRED VENUS

SIZE: 1 to 1 inches long

Venus clams are named for the Greek goddess Venus, who was graceful and beautiful. There are many of these shells in some places on the southern coast, especially in northwestern Florida. Two kinds of Venus shells commonly found from North Carolina to Florida are the **Sunray Venus** and the **Cross-Barred Venus**. The Cross-Barred Venus is less than 2 inches long. It is shaped like a rounded triangle and has eight to nine concentric ridges

SUNRAY VENUS

SIZE: 3 to 6 inches long

curving around its shell from the hinge to the outer edge. They are mostly white inside and out (the outside can be slightly yellow or gray). Rust-colored rays curve across the shell, starting at the hinge; on some shells, the rays go all the way to the outer edge.

TURKEY WING

SIZE: 3 inches long

The **Turkey Wing** is a type of clam shell. It has two other names, Noah's Ark and Zebra Ark. All of these names describe it well. The shell looks like a boat when the animal is alive and attached to a rock. Each of the two shells is shaped like a turkey wing, and it is decorated with reddish-brown stripes that look like a zebra. The inside of the shell is pale purple with many marks that look like teeth.

ANGEL WING

SIZE: 8 inches long

If you find both halves of an angel wing's shell, you can easily see how this shell got its name. When the shell is opened flat, it looks like a pair of angel wings. The **False Angel Wing** and its close cousin, called the Fallen Angel Wing or, simply, the **Angel Wing**, are similar in shape. But the False Angel Wing is much smaller. Both are beautiful, thin, white shells. They are long and narrow with ribs that run from the hinge to the outer edge of the shell. The ribs are bigger on an Angel Wing than on a False Angel Wing. Both live in mud.

FALSE ANGEL WING

SIZE: 2 inches long

BLOOD ARK

SIZE: 1 $^1/_8$ to 3 inches long

The **Blood Ark** got its name because, unlike other mollusks, it has red blood. Its shell is thick, with twenty-six or more wide ribs. It is white, but may have a fuzzy, brown covering on the outside. It lives in the sand or mud.

PONDEROUS ARK

SIZE: 2 inches long

When the **Ponderous Ark** is alive, it has a velvety dark covering on the outside. When it is not alive, the sturdy, round shell is mostly white. You can count between twenty-seven and thirty-one ribs on the outside. Inside, there are many little dents that look like teeth.

COCKLE SHELL

Cockles are thick and rounded shells. Two small cockles are found along the Atlantic Coast from Maine to North Carolina. They are called **Morton's Cockle** and the **Northern Dwarf Cockle**. Morton's Cockle is tan or white with brown, zigzag stripes. The Northern Dwarf Cockle is white with tan markings. It has wide ribs running from the hinge to the outside edge of the shell. The **Giant Atlantic Cockle** is the largest cockle on the Atlantic Coast; it lives farther south than the Morton's and Northern Dwarf cockles. It is tan or yellow with brown markings on the outside and pink or yellow on the inside. It has thick ribs like those of the Northern Dwarf Cockle.

GIANT ATLANTIC COCKLE

SIZE: 2 ¹/₄ to 5 ¹/₄ inches across

MORTON'S COCKLE

SIZE: 2 ¹/₄ to 5 ¹/₄ inches across

NORTHERN DWARF COCKLE

SIZE: $^1/_2$ inch across

STRAWBERRY COCKLE

SIZE: 1 to 3 inches across

YELLOW COCKLE

SIZE: 2 inches across

The **Strawberry Cockle** is cream-colored with speckles of reddish brown. It has thirty-three to thirty-six ridges running from the outer edge to the hinge of the shell. **Yellow Cockles** are usually yellow inside and out; they have thirty to forty ridges.

NORTHERN CARDITA

SIZE: 1 1/2 inches long

The **Northern Cardita** is a small, but thick, shell with about twenty ribs on the outside. It is white and smooth on the inside and brown on the outside. It lives in sand or mud.

CLAMS

The **Atlantic Jackknife Clam** and **Atlantic Razor Clam** are named for their shapes and their sharp edges. (They are not sharp enough to cut you.) Both shells are shiny and greenish on the outside and white on the inside. The Razor Clam is round on the ends, and the Jackknife Clam looks more like a rectangle. Both shells are thin and fragile. You should carry the shells of these two animals carefully, so that they will not break.

ATLANTIC JACKKNIFE CLAM

SIZE: 3 to 8 inches long

ATLANTIC RAZOR CLAM

SIZE: 1 $\frac{1}{2}$ to 2 $\frac{5}{8}$ inches long

The tiny **Atlantic Nut Clam** is shaped like a triangle. It is shiny white, like a pearl, on the inside, and white with brownish green "skin" on the outside. Look for this shell in the sand or the mud.

ATLANTIC NUT CLAM

SIZE: $^1/_2$ inch long

The **Atlantic Surf Clam** is the largest clam on the East Coast. Starfish and other sea creatures like to eat this clam, but it can sometimes jump to safety by using its big, strong foot. People like to eat this clam, too. The Atlantic Surf Clam is mostly white with some yellow on the outside. It is shaped like a triangle with rounded angles. This clam lives in the surf, where the waves break against the shore. It is found along many Atlantic Coast beaches. This clam has several names, depending on where it lives. In Maine, for instance, it is sometimes called the Hen Clam. In some other places, it is known as the Beach Clam.

ATLANTIC SURF CLAM

SIZE: 6 inches long

FILE YOLDIA

SIZE: 2 to 2 $^1/_2$ inches long

The **File Yoldia** is a delicate and fancy clam shell. It is green on the outside and bluish white on the inside. Along the hinge side of the shell, the edge is rough, like a file. One end of the shell is rounded; the other is lightly pointed.

SOFT-SHELL CLAM

SIZE: 3 inches long

The **Soft-Shell Clam** is another clam that people like to eat. In fact, it is often called the Steamer Clam because of the way it is cooked. This clam lives in the mud. You may see a living Soft-Shell Clam squirt water up through the mud at low tide. If you see holes in the mud or wet sand, look for some empty shells nearby. The Soft-Shell Clam is smaller, longer, and not as wide as the Atlantic Surf Clam. It is white, like chalk, inside and out.

QUAHOG

The **Northern Quahog** (pronounced KO-hog) has many different names: Hard-shell Clam, Cherrystone Clam, and Littleneck. Indians made the shell of the quahog into tools and jewelry. They also used pieces of this shell, which they called wampum, as money, to trade for items that they needed or wanted.

Along some parts of the coast, people like to eat quahogs. Adult quahogs are about half the size of an adult Atlantic Surf Clam. The Northern Quahog is grayish yellow on the outside and white and shiny inside. Sometimes a light purple muscle scar can be found on the inside. The **Ocean Quahog** is more rounded than the Northern Quahog, and its shell is thicker. It is white inside and out but might be covered with a thin, black "skin." (See the introduction to this chapter.)

NORTHERN QUAHOG

SIZE: 2 3/4 to 4 1/4 inches across

OCEAN QUAHOG

SIZE: 3 to 5 inches across

MUSSEL

In Chapter 2, "Sea Creatures," you can find out about living mussels.

The **Atlantic Ribbed Mussel** is easy to identify because of the ribs on its shell that run from the hinge to the outer edge. It is grayish-white on the outside, with brown "skin," and light blue on the inside.

ATLANTIC RIBBED MUSSEL

SIZE: 2 to 5 inches long

BLUE MUSSEL

SIZE: 1 ¼ to 4 inches long

The **Blue Mussel** has a shell that is light blue on the inside and gray on the outside, with a dark blue "skin." You can see curved growth rings on the outside of this shell. In some places, the Blue Mussel is a popular seafood.

NORTHERN HORSE MUSSEL

SIZE: 2 to 9 inches long

The **Northern Horse Mussel** has a large, oval shell that is thicker than that of the Blue Mussel. It is light purple on the outside but is usually covered with brown "skin," it is gray on the inside. Like the Blue Mussel, it has growth lines on the outside.

85

OYSTER

Oysters are like snowflakes; it's hard to find two exactly alike. Their shapes vary, depending upon where and how they live. Still, it is easy to identify an oyster because no other shell looks like it. The shell is very rough and bumpy on the outside, like the **Eastern Oyster**, and shiny smooth on the inside. Its color is dirty white or yellowish on the outside. Inside, a dark purple or black muscle scar remains where the body was attached. Oysters live in the shallow water of bays and saltwater rivers. Empty oyster shells are often found on the beach.

EASTERN OYSTER

SIZE: 5 inches long

SCALLOP

Scallops are a favorite seafood for many people, and they are popular with shell collectors because of their beautiful shells. A scallop shell is easy to identify. They are almost flat and mostly round, with a straight edge at the hinge. There are thin ribs running from the hinge to the outer edge. The **Atlantic Deep Sea Scallop** can be as big as a dinner plate. It is tan or brown on the outside. The **Atlantic Bay Scallop** is much smaller. It is gray, yellowish, or red-brown on the outside. Both scallops are white on the inside.

ATLANTIC BAY SCALLOP

SIZE: 3 inches across

ATLANTIC DEEP SEA SCALLOP

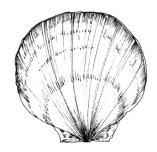

SIZE: 8 inches across

PEN SHELL

These shells look more like fans than pens. They are nearly flat, wide at the top, and pointed at the opposite end. Some pen shells are orange; others are dark-colored, greenish brown. The **Stiff Pen Shell** has ridges that run along the length of the shell. The **Saw-Toothed Pen Shell** is not quite as flat and is smoother, with many fine ridges along the upper edge. Pen shells are delicate and break easily so it might be difficult to find a whole one.

SAW-TOOTHED PEN SHELL

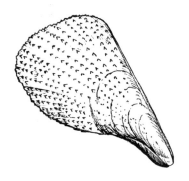

SIZE: 6 to 12 inches long

STIFF PEN SHELL

SIZE: 5 to 10 inches long

4 ❃ INSECTS

Most of the insects listed below are found inland as well as on the coast. Except for the grasshopper and the cricket, avoid these creatures because they bite or sting.

EASTERN SAND WASP

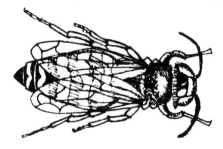

COLOR: *black with yellow stripes*
SIZE: *¹/₂ inch long*

The **Eastern Sand Wasp** can be found throughout North America, but it is especially common on sand dunes and beaches. Its body is black with pale yellow stripes. It has bright yellow legs.

DEER FLY

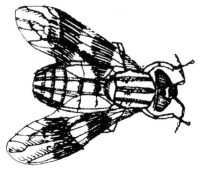

COLOR: *black with light green*
SIZE: *$^3/_8$ to $^5/_8$ inch long*

Deer Flies like to bite deer, but they can be a real pest to people, too. They live in woodlands and meadows but are often seen along the seashore, especially if there are woods nearby. They give a painful bite as soon as they land on their victim. The body is black with light green markings. A Deer Fly is easy to recognize by its wings, which have black bands and make a triangle shape when the insect is not flying.

AMERICAN HORSE FLY

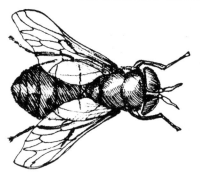

COLOR: *black with green eyes*
SIZE: *$^3/_4$ to 1 inch long*

The **American Horse Fly** is another insect with a mean bite. It is sometimes called a "Green Head" because of its large green eyes, which make this insect easy to identify. It is often seen on beaches and salt marshes.

90

SALTMARSH MOSQUITO

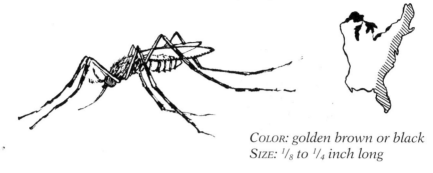

COLOR: golden brown or black
SIZE: $\frac{1}{8}$ to $\frac{1}{4}$ inch long

Saltmarsh Mosquitoes are like all North American mosquitoes except that they prefer to live near salt water. They can be golden brown or black.

TICK

The tick that you might find on your dog or cat will sometimes bite people, but the bite, although it can hurt and itch, is not harmful to most people. There is a smaller tick, however, whose bite can cause a serious illness called Lyme Disease. This tick has different names in different parts of the United States. It is sometimes called a **Deer Tick**, a Bear Tick, or a Sheep Tick.

DEER TICK

COLOR: dark brown
SIZE: $\frac{1}{16}$ inch long

DOG TICK

COLOR: dark brown
SIZE: ¹/₈ inch long

All ticks have eight legs, like a spider. Deer Ticks are found along the seashore and inland in tall grass, bushes, and in the woods. Ticks don't fly but they often fall on people when the wind blows the insects out of trees and bushes. They can also crawl on you if you sit down on a log or in the grass.

To prevent being bitten by a tick, wear long pants tucked into your socks when you walk in the woods or in tall grass. Also, wear a hat and a long-sleeved shirt. It is best to wear light-colored clothing so that you can see a tick if it lands or crawls on you. Place a blanket or some other covering on the ground before sitting down.

The symptoms of Lyme Disease can include a rash, headache, sore or stiff muscles or joints, a fever, swollen glands, or red, itchy eyes. If the disease is not treated it can lead to more severe symptoms, such as heart problems or arthritis. Lyme Disease can be treated with antibiotics. If you find a tick stuck in your skin, ask an adult to help you remove it and take it to a doctor or a nature center where an expert can identify it.

SEASIDE GRASSHOPPER

COLOR: light brown or gray with small black spots; light yellow back wings
SIZE: 1 to 1 ¼ inches long

The **Seaside Grasshopper** is as likely to be found resting in the sand among the dunes as hopping in the grass. It has knobby knees and bulging eyes like the grasshoppers you may see in your yard.

FIELD CRICKET

COLOR: black or dark brown
SIZE: ½ to 1 inch long

Another great hopper, this insect was made famous by Pinocchio's conscience, Jiminy Cricket. It is shaped much like a grasshopper, but smaller. A **Field Cricket** has a very big voice for its size. Listen for three loud chirps in the tall grass. If you live where it gets cold in the autumn, you will probably hear a cricket in your house. They come inside to get warm.

5 ☆ SHOREBIRDS

At first, it might seem that identifying birds is a lot harder than identifying a shell in your hand or a plant that's growing in the ground. But each bird has its own color and shape; with a little practice, you will find that many birds are easy to identify. The pattern and coloring of a bird's feathers are called its field marks. The *field marks* to look for are included in the descriptions that follow. The size shown for each bird is the length of an adult bird from the tip of its bill to the tip of its tail.

The **Great Blue Heron** is easy to identify because it is so big. It stands more than three feet tall, and has wings that reach nearly seven feet from tip to tip. The Great Blue Heron is the largest shorebird on the Atlantic Coast. Its body and wings are gray-blue; its head and the front of its long neck are mostly white. It has an orange bill and long yellow legs.

GREAT BLUE HERON

BODY LENGTH: *3 feet, 2 inches*
WINGSPAN: *almost 7 feet*

Look for this bird standing tall in marsh grass or at the edge of a quiet cove. When it's looking for food, the Great Blue Heron stands so still that it sometimes looks like a long stick poking out of the water. When it spots something to eat—a fish, shrimp, or bug—the bird's long neck snaps forward, and the heron grabs its *prey* with its sharp beak. When it flies, the Great Blue Heron folds its neck into the shape of the letter S and lets its long legs trail behind. You might see Great Blue herons in streams, rivers, ponds, and lakes, as well as along the coast.

GREAT WHITE EGRET

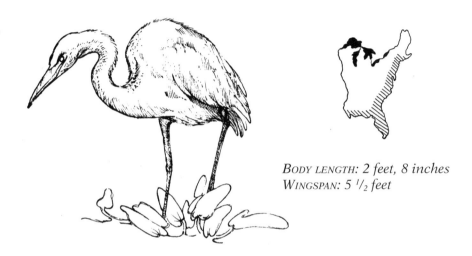

BODY LENGTH: 2 feet, 8 inches
WINGSPAN: 5 ¹/₂ feet

Not long ago, egrets were hunted for their beautiful white feathers, which were used to decorate fancy hats. Now the birds are protected from hunters by law, and they can be seen in many places along the Atlantic Coast. Egrets are members of the heron family. They like the same foods, and they hunt and live in the same places— shallow, marshy coves and inlets. The **Great White Egret** is smaller than its relative, the Great Blue Heron. Its feathers are pure white, its bill bright yellow, and its legs and feet are shiny black.

SNOWY EGRET

BODY LENGTH: 20 inches
WINGSPAN: 3 feet

   The **Snowy Egret** is all white, too. It is about half the size of a Great Blue Heron. It has a black bill, black legs, and bright-yellow feet.

SANDPIPER

There are many kinds of sandpipers. Most sandpipers seen on the Atlantic Coast have tan backs, white bellies, and dark spots on their breasts. Compared to other shorebirds, most sandpipers are small—about the size of a sparrow. However, their legs are longer than a sparrow's, and they have long, thin bills that they use to catch tiny sea creatures along the edge of the water.

It's fun to watch sandpipers feed because they look like windup toys. They run so fast you can hardly see their legs. Their heads and tails bob up and down, and they all move together, like dancers on a stage.

LEAST SANDPIPER

BODY LENGTH: 5 inches
WINGSPAN: 11 inches

Look for the **Least Sandpiper** along the muddy edges of rivers and salt marshes. It is brown on top and has a streaked breast and white belly. It has a dark brown bill, a white stripe above its eyes, and yellow legs. Even though it is called the Least Sandpiper, it is one of the most common sandpipers in the United States.

PURPLE SANDPIPER

BODY LENGTH: 8 inches
WINGSPAN: 17 inches

The **Purple Sandpiper** is not really purple. Its back and breast are streaked dark gray and white. Its belly is white, and it has yellow legs and a yellow bill with a black point. Purple Sandpipers are common in rocky places all along the Atlantic Coast.

SANDERLING

BODY LENGTH: 7 inches
WINGSPAN: 14 inches

Sanderlings are often seen on sandy beaches at the edge of the water. This sandpiper has a white breast, a black bill, and black legs. In summer, its back and breast are tan with dark gray streaks; in winter, its back is light gray with dark gray streaks.

SEMIPALMATED SANDPIPER

BODY LENGTH: 6 inches
WINGSPAN: 12 inches

The **Semipalmated Sandpiper** is one of the most common shorebirds on the Atlantic Coast. It looks like the Least Sandpiper, but its body is gray on top and it has black legs. It also has a black bill.

SPOTTED SANDPIPER

BODY LENGTH: 7 inches
WINGSPAN: 15 inches

The **Spotted Sandpiper** is common all along the Atlantic Coast. It has a brown back and brown wings. There is a white stripe above each eye. In summer, its white breast and belly are covered with dark spots. It has yellow legs and a yellow bill with a black point. This is one of the few sandpipers that is often seen alone.

TERN

   Terns are slender, fast-flying shorebirds. When looking for food, a tern flies with its sharp bill pointed down.
If it sees a fish or bug in the water below, the tern dives
straight down to snatch its prey from the water. There are
several kinds of terns that you might see along the Atlantic Coast. They look so much alike that even expert bird
watchers sometimes have trouble telling them apart. They
all have tails shaped like the letter V. They have white
bodies; narrow gray wings; long, sharp bills and black
caps on their heads. They are all about the same size, but
they are also different in some ways.

CASPIAN TERN

BODY LENGTH: 20 inches
WINGSPAN: 4 feet, 4 inches

   The **Caspian Tern** is the largest of the terns described
in this book. It is shaped more like a gull than other terns,
and it has a bright red bill and black feet.

COMMON TERN

BODY LENGTH: 14 inches
WINGSPAN: 2 feet

The **Common Tern's** wings are longer than its tail. The tail is dark gray along the outside edge and the wings are dark gray on the tips. The Common Tern has a bright, red-orange bill (sometimes with a black tip) and feet the same color.

FORSTER'S TERN

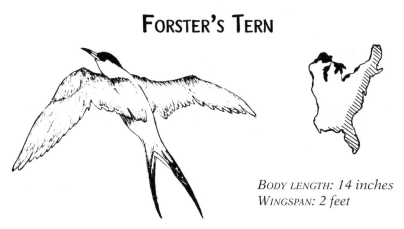

BODY LENGTH: 14 inches
WINGSPAN: 2 feet

The **Forster's Tern** looks a lot like the Common Tern, but its tail is light gray with a darker gray band along the inside of the V. It has yellow-orange feet and a yellow-orange bill with a black point. The Forster's Tern is easiest to identify in the winter, when it has a narrow, black patch around its eyes. This tern is most often seen in salt marshes.

Roseate Tern

Body Length: 15 inches
Wingspan: 2 feet

The **Roseate Tern** has an all-white tail. Just the opposite of the Common Tern, the Roseate Tern's tail is longer than its wings. The Roseate Tern has a black bill and orange feet.

Gull

The most common gulls along the Atlantic Coast are the Herring Gull, the Great Black-Backed Gull, and the Laughing Gull. Like other gulls, they are strong birds with long wings, webbed feet, and a strong, hooked bill. They will eat anything from fish that they catch in the water to peanut-butter sandwiches and potato chips left by picnickers. They hang around anywhere they can grab a snack—the beach, a fish pier, even garbage dumps.

Gulls have a trick for eating food that has a hard shell, like a crab or a clam. After the bird grabs its prey from the rocks or the sand, it flies up in the air and drops the prey on the rocks to break the shell. Then the gull can easily get to the soft meat inside. Gulls are most beautiful, though, when soaring like a glider on the ocean breeze.

GREAT BLACK-BACKED GULL

BODY LENGTH: 2 feet
WINGSPAN: 5 feet, 5 inches

HERRING GULL

BODY LENGTH: 20 inches
WINGSPAN: 4 feet

The **Great Black-Backed Gull** and the **Herring Gull** are often seen together. Both are snowy white, except for their backs and the tops of their wings. They both have pale pink legs and a yellow bill with a red spot on the bottom. But it is easy to tell them apart. The Herring Gull has a gray back and gray wings with black tips. The Great Black-Backed Gull has a black back and wings and it is larger than the Herring Gull. When these two birds have an argument, the Great Black-Backed Gull always wins!

If you see many of these gulls together, you may see some gull-sized birds that are the color of mud. These are not different kinds of gulls. They are just young Herring or Great Black-Backed gulls. Like some other gulls, these birds do not get their full adult colors until they are two or three years old.

LAUGHING GULL

BODY LENGTH: 13 inches
WINGSPAN: 3 feet, 5 inches

You can identify the **Laughing Gull** with your eyes closed. Its loud ha-ha-ha-ha-ha can be heard all along the Atlantic Coast. But even when the Laughing Gull is not "laughing," it is easy to identify. It has a black head; a white rim around its eyes; and a snow-white breast, neck, and belly. Its bill and feet are dark orange. The Laughing Gull has a gray back and wings, but it is smaller than Herring and Great Black-Backed gulls. Young Laughing Gulls have brown backs and wings and tan heads. The very young birds have a wide black band along the top edge of their tails.

106

PELICAN

The pelican doesn't laugh; in fact, it rarely makes a sound. But it is an amusing bird to watch. It has an enormous bill; the bottom half has a large pouch for carrying fish, and it looks like it is smiling—a very large smile. Pelicans have large wings for the size of their bodies and they are powerful fliers.

AMERICAN WHITE PELICAN

BODY LENGTH: 5 feet
WINGSPAN: 9 feet

This bird can't be confused with its brown cousin. It is pure white with black wing feathers and has an orange bill, legs, and feet. (Young **American White Pelicans** have gray bills and a gray neck.) Unlike its relative the Brown Pelican, this bird does not dive to get its food. American White Pelicans feed by swimming slowly along in shallow water, scooping up fish with their large bills. Sometimes several White Pelicans fish together, forming a V just as they (and other birds) do when they migrate.

BROWN PELICAN

BODY LENGTH: 3 ¹/₂ feet
WINGSPAN: 7 feet

The **Brown Pelican** is commonly seen along the southern coast, sitting on bridges, piers, buoys, and the tops of telephone poles. They often fly along just a few inches above the water or in a line of other pelicans looking for fish in the water. When a Brown Pelican dives for food, it drops straight down into the water as if it had been shot from the sky. In some places they are quite tame and stay close to people, begging for food.

The Brown Pelican has a light-brown body and a white neck and head. In the summer, look for a dark red stripe along the back of its neck. The bill is gray and light orange. A young Brown Pelican has a white body with light brown wings and neck.

Double-Crested Cormorant

BODY LENGTH: *2 feet, 4 inches*
WINGSPAN: *4 feet*

Fishermen call these birds "shags," perhaps because of the shaggy crest on top of their heads. The cormorant is a very good diver and underwater swimmer. It uses its wings and webbed feet to "fly" through the water chasing after fish, its favorite food. You might have trouble getting a good look at this bird during feeding time. One minute the cormorant is floating along on the surface of the water, its head pointed up as if it were afraid of getting its bill wet. The next minute it disappears. It might be out of sight for several minutes before it pops to the surface, often far away from the spot where it dived.

Cormorants are friendly birds (with each other, that is), and you might see a large flock of them on the rocks offshore. They often sit with their wings stretched out to dry. Cormorants must dry their wings that way because they do not have natural oil in their feathers to shed water as other water birds do.

The **Double-Crested Cormorant** is a large bird—about the size of a goose. The double crest on its head is hard to see, but this bird is not hard to identify. It has greenish-black feathers, black feet, a gray bill, and an orange patch on its chin.

COMMON LOON

BODY LENGTH: 2 feet
WINGSPAN: 4 feet

Beginning bird watchers sometimes confuse the **Common Loon** with the cormorant. They are about the same size, and both birds sit low in the water with their heads pointed up. Both are very good divers and swimmers. In the winter, a young Double-Crested Cormorant has almost the same coloring as a loon does. But there are ways to tell them apart. With its legs far back on its body, a loon is made for swimming, not walking. Unlike the cormorant, the loon hardly ever is seen on land.

In late spring, summer, and early fall, the loon is easily identified by its summer colors—a dark green head, a striped "collar," and rows of white spots on its dark back. The Common Loon spends the summer on lakes and ponds, where it is often heard at night making the spooky, laughing sound that gave this bird its name. The Common Loon really has four different calls that it uses to "talk" with other loons. During fall and winter, when the loon is seen most often on the coast, it is usually quiet.

MALLARD

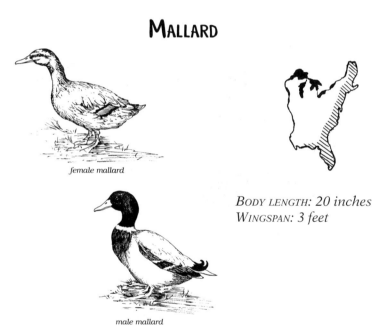

female mallard

male mallard

BODY LENGTH: 20 inches
WINGSPAN: 3 feet

The **Mallard** duck is another bird that lives on lakes and ponds as well as along the coast. You might see Mallards in a marsh or shallow cove, paddling along in a group made up of Mallards and other ducks. Mallards are often seen with their close cousin, the American Black Duck.

111

The male Mallard is easiest to identify. It has a shiny, green head; white neck band; rust-colored breast; white belly; and tan wings with a bright-blue stripe. (The stripe looks like a blue patch when the Mallard is sitting in the water.) The female looks a lot like the American Black Duck, but she is a lighter shade of brown. Also, her wing stripe is blue like the male Mallard, not purple like the stripe of the American Black Duck.

AMERICAN BLACK DUCK

BODY LENGTH: 18 inches
WINGSPAN: 3 feet

You might have to get up early in the morning to see this bird. The **American Black Duck** is very shy (perhaps because it's a popular target for duck hunters), and it usually eats and travels at night. Still, the American-Black Duck is the most common wild duck on the Atlantic

Coast. If you can visit a *bird sanctuary* along the coast, you are very likely to see an American Black Duck eating during the daytime.

The American Black Duck is really dark brown, with a lighter brown head. It looks so similar to a female Mallard that it is often called the Dusky Mallard or Black Mallard. The American Black Duck is the same size as a Mallard and even has the same loud quack. But you can identify the American Black Duck by its bright yellow bill and by the purple band with the narrow, white stripe it has along its wing. Both the male and the female have yellow bills, but the male's is a brighter yellow.

Mallards and American Black Ducks are "surface feeders." They eat plants and sometimes bugs and small fish that they find on or near the surface of the water. These birds can be a funny sight while feeding. You might see one of these ducks paddling along, nibbling at the surface of the water. Suddenly it dips its head and the front of its body into the water to reach for food, leaving its tail sticking up in the air.

The **Bufflehead** is one of the smallest ducks on the Atlantic Coast. Its markings make it easy to identify. The male Bufflehead is snowy white on its breast, stomach, and sides. It has a white patch, like a cap, that stretches from eye to eye on top of its dark green head. The top of its wings and body are black with white stripes. It is easiest to see the stripes when the bird is flying. The female Bufflehead is grayish white on the breast, stomach, and sides. She is dark gray everywhere else, but has a white patch on each cheek and a white band at the back of each wing near her body. Like other sea ducks, the Bufflehead

BUFFLEHEAD

BODY LENGTH: 12 inches
WINGSPAN: 2 feet

has a plump body, a short neck, and a short tail. Winter is the best time to see this bird on the coast, because it stays near lakes and rivers in the summer. In the winter, you often see large flocks of Buffleheads in saltwater rivers and in coves.

This is the most common goose, not only along the Atlantic Coast, but in all of North America. The **Canada Goose** is large and it is easy to identify by the color and pattern of its feathers. Look for a gray body; a long, black neck, and a white band, which looks like a wide strap, under the goose's chin.

Like many birds, Canada Geese migrate. They fly to cooler places in the spring and to warmer places in the fall. Canada Geese migrate in groups (flocks)—from a few dozen birds to one hundred or more. When flying, the flock forms the letter V in the air. You can often hear the geese coming before you see them, because they honk as if trying to get through a traffic jam. When they stop to

CANADA GOOSE

BODY LENGTH: 2 to 3 feet
WINGSPAN: 5 feet

rest, they often can be seen in fields near the water, grazing on grass just as cows do.

This large, fish-eating *raptor* might be seen anywhere along the Atlantic Coast, but it is most commonly seen in Florida, where it lives all year. Farther north, it is a summer resident. It also lives near lakes and rivers—anywhere the fishing is good. When the **Osprey** is flying, its tail is shaped like a fan, and the tips of its long wings (five and a half feet from tip to tip) are separated like fingers. The bird is white underneath and brown on top. Its head is white, but a brown streak runs from its beak to its neck.

This majestic bird, our national bird and emblem, is a thrilling sight to see. With a wingspan of nearly seven feet, a **Bald Eagle** seems to fill the sky with its silent, graceful flight. They often soar very high with their wings spread flat. When hunting for food, they fly closer to the ground.

OSPREY

BODY LENGTH: 22 inches
WINGSPAN: 5 feet

Bald Eagles are *predators* that eat rodents and other small
animals, as well as fish. Like the Osprey, the Bald Eagle
is a raptor with strong claws called talons that it uses to
capture and carry its food.

Bald Eagles mate for life. The ones that migrate usually return to the same nest year after year. Their nests are
enormous and can weigh as much as a ton.

It is easy to identify a Bald Eagle by its white head and
tail, dark brown body, and yellow beak and feet. This
bird is not really bald. The "bald" is from the word "pie-
bald," which describes an animal that has two distinctly
different colors—one light and the other dark. In this
case, it refers to the bird's snow-white head and tail that
contrast sharply with its dark brown body.

BALD EAGLE

BODY LENGTH: 32 inches
WINGSPAN: 6 to 7 ¹/₂ feet

The Bald Eagle was once endangered because there were *pesticides* in the fish it eats. A chemical in the pesticides called DDT changed the bird's body chemistry so that the eggs it laid had very thin shells that broke before the baby birds hatched. Since DDT has been banned to protect the environment, the eggs are hatching and there are more Bald Eagles on the Atlantic Coast and elsewhere than there were 20 years ago.

The Bald Eagle can be seen in every state in America except Hawaii. More than half of its total population of about 70,000 lives in Alaska. On the Atlantic Coast, they are commonly seen in Florida, where they live all year, but in the warmer months, spring through early fall, they can be seen all along the East Coast.

There is an interesting Web site devoted to the Bald Eagle. It is listed in Appendix A.

RED-WINGED BLACKBIRD

BODY LENGTH: 8 inches
WINGSPAN: 14 inches

This cheerful blackbird seems to sing every time it lands and takes off—a loud, long, musical but slightly squeaky song that is easy to recognize. Like many birds, the male has brightly colored feathers, but the female does not. The male **Red-Winged Blackbird** has reddish-orange and yellow patches on its shoulders. With its brown feathers and streaked breast, the female looks like a large sparrow. Both the male and the female have black feet. The Red-Winged Blackbird is a familiar sight throughout the United States, but it is most common in marshlands and in fields that are near water.

SEASIDE SPARROW

BODY LENGTH: 6 inches
WINGSPAN: 7 inches

This is the only sparrow that lives only near the seashore. It is commonly seen in salt marshes and bushes along the Atlantic Coast from New England to Florida. It is a perky little bird, mostly gray, with a white throat and a long yellow patch in front of each eye. The male and the female have the same coloring. The **Seaside Sparrow** has a short, narrow tail and a long, gray bill that it uses to catch insects and small sea creatures, such as tiny crabs and snails.

6 ✳ SEASHORE PLANTS

IN THE SEA

The ocean has beautiful gardens of plants, commonly called seaweed. Sea animals need seaweed, just as land animals need land plants. Seaweed provides food and shelter.

Land plants use roots to get food and water and stay in the soil. But seaweed does not have roots. Seaweed has a holdfast, which looks like a root. The *holdfast* keeps the seaweed attached to rocks or shells even when the sea is rough. If you try to pull the holdfast loose, you will see why it is called a holdfast.

Seaweeds have been used for food, garden fertilizer, and even medicine in many parts of the world for thousands of years. In some places, too much seaweed has been harvested (taken live from the ocean). This can hurt the balance of plant and animal life in the surrounding area and can cause *erosion*. One of the Web sites listed in Appendix A tells how to safely harvest seaweed; there are also some recipes for cooking with seaweed. In this chapter, several seaweeds are described as being good to eat, but check with an adult before sampling any wild-growing plant.

There are many different types and colors of seaweed. Seaweed that lives near the surface of the water is green. Brown, red, and purple seaweeds are found in deeper, colder water. Sometimes you can see it growing along the water's edge, but many kinds are left on the beach by the tide, especially after a storm.

GREEN THREAD ALGAE

COLOR: *bright green*
SIZE: *2 feet tall*

Alga is the Latin word for seaweed, which makes sense because all seaweeds are algae. Algae are simple plants that have no stems or roots. Most algae live in water. **Green Thread Algae** grows in tide pools and in salt marshes. You also might see it on boat docks and buoys. In Florida it grows on the roots of mangrove trees. On the

beach you might find it attached to shells or other debris
that have been washed up by ocean waves. Green Thread
Algae grows in big clumps, tangled up, and looks some-

ROCKWEED

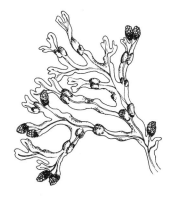

COLOR: brown
SIZE: up to 3 feet tall

thing like green spaghetti that has been cooked too long.
Low tide is the best time to get a close look at the brown
seaweed known as **Rockweed**. It has many flat branches,
each with a rib in the middle. The branches are covered
with pairs of oval-shaped pods. These pods are called
"air bladders" (Rockweed is sometimes called Bladder
Wrack). The air bladders are like little water wings that
help the seaweed float on the surface of the water. This
seaweed needs to stay on the surface to get sunlight.
Large beds of Rockweed cover the rocks in many places
on the coast.

Knotted Wrack

Color: brown
Size: up to 2 feet tall

Knotted Wrack looks like its close relative, the Knotted Rockweed. The branches of Knotted Wrack, however, are thinner and have no rib in the center. The air bladders on the Knotted Wrack grow singly on the branches, rather than in pairs. In the winter, small, round, yellow, leaf-like bumps grow along the branches. This seaweed is found in calm water and on rocks in salt marshes. Knotted Wrack is sometimes called Yellow Tang or Sea Whistle.

Kelp

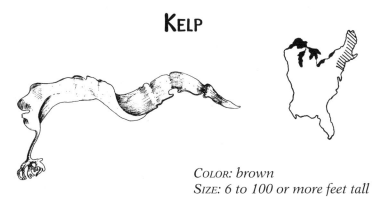

Color: brown
Size: 6 to 100 or more feet tall

With its long, flat, wide blade, **Kelp** is easy to identify. The blade has a long stem, like a tail, with a holdfast on the end. Kelp can grow very fast, nearly a foot a day in some parts of the world. This seaweed grows where the ocean is cold and can be seen in mussel beds and under docks. When you find Kelp on the beach, the holdfast might still be attached to a mussel shell.

DULSE

COLOR: *brown or dark red*
SIZE: *20 inches tall*

This large-leafed seaweed is a popular food in some places. It can be dried and added as a seasoning to soups and salad dressings, or it can be eaten in dried pieces that are something like potato chips. If you find a piece of **Dulse** growing among the rocks or lying on the beach, you might not think it looks or feels very tasty. It is brown or dark red and feels like leather. Dulse often grows on, or near, Kelp.

Sea Colander

Color: brown
Size: 1 ¹/₂ feet tall

Here is another seaweed with a wide blade that is found along the New England coast and farther north. But this one is full of holes. That is why it is called a colander. (A colander is a pot with holes that is used to drain water from pasta or vegetables after they are cooked.) The brown blade of the **Sea Colander** has a thick rib in the middle. The blade of the Sea Colander is shorter and wider than a Kelp blade, and the stem is much shorter. The Sea Colander is sometimes called Devil's Apron.

Sea Lettuce, also called Green Laver, looks like other lettuce. It has flat, thin, green leaves that are wavy on the edges. These leaves can grow to be two feet long, but the leaves are so thin and delicate that you usually find much smaller pieces of it on the beach. You may see it growing in quiet coves and salt marshes all along the Atlantic Coast. Like other lettuce, Sea Lettuce can be eaten. Remember: Never eat any plant you find outside without washing it thoroughly and checking with an adult.

126

Sea Lettuce

Color: green
Size: 1 to 2 feet tall

Purple Laver

Color: purple, pink, red,
or brown
Size: 6 inches tall

Purple Laver is a popular food in some places, especially in Japan, where it is wrapped around rice or fish, put in soup, or eaten by itself. As you might guess, Purple Laver is closely related to Green Laver, but it is, of course, a different color. Although it is called purple, it may be pink, reddish, or brownish. Like Green Laver, it has flat, thin leaves that are wavy on the edges. It grows where the water is calm, in large beds, or colonies, attached to rocks or other seaweeds.

SEA GRASS

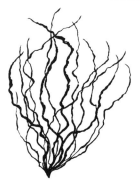

COLOR: green
SIZE: up to 6 feet tall

This seaweed looks like grass that needs to be ironed. It has long wrinkled green blades that may be a foot or more tall. **Sea Grass**, sometimes called Maiden Hair, grows on rocks all along the coast from Canada to South Carolina.

LINK CONFETTI

COLOR: green
SIZE: 2 to 3 feet tall

Link Confetti, another kind of sea grass, can be found as far south as Florida. It is bright green, and its hollow blades have air bubbles that look like bumps. Link Confetti sea grass is taller than its cousin, the Sea Grass, and it can grow where the water is muddy and dirty.

IRISH MOSS

COLOR: *purple, red, reddish, green, or yellowish white*
SIZE: *2 to 4 inches tall*

This seaweed is called **Irish Moss**, because it also grows in Ireland. There it was used for cooking and medicine long before Columbus discovered America. It is also eaten in New England, where it is found all along the coast. Many New England cookbooks have a recipe for pudding made with Irish Moss. This plant is small, with many flat branches.

CHENILLE WEED

COLOR: *bright red*
SIZE: *up to 2 feet tall*

Chenille Weed is a beautiful red plant with many branches. The branches and stem are covered with soft furry-looking leaves. It grows underwater in protected places on the Atlantic Coast.

SEA POTATO

COLOR: dark green or yellowish brown
SIZE: 1 to 3 inches long

The **Sea Potato** looks more like cauliflower than a potato. It also looks a little like a brain, which is why it is sometimes called Rat's Brain. It grows in clumps that feel like a sponge. The clumps are hollow inside. Because it is hollow, it floats in the water. The Sea Potato is often found attached to Irish Moss or another seaweed.

NEAR THE SEA

Only special plants can live in the salty air of the seashore. The many flowers, plants, and grasses that grow along the Atlantic Coast must be able to live in cold and hot weather and to survive ocean storms and strong winds. The grasses of the seashore are a pretty sight sprouting from salt marshes and beaches. But they are much more than that. On beaches and dunes, grasses keep the sand from blowing away and help prevent erosion. In the salt marsh, grasses make safe nesting and feeding places for many birds and other creatures. When you explore the dunes, stay on paths or walkways, and be careful not to walk on the fragile grasses.

EELGRASS

COLOR: green
SIZE: 3 to 4 feet tall

This grass lives in salt water, but it is not a seaweed. Its roots are buried in the sand or mud beneath the water. You can see its long, flat, green leaves, waving like ribbons near the surface of shallow coves and rivers, all along the Atlantic Coast. **Eelgrass** makes a good hiding place for crabs, fishes, and other sea creatures.

TURTLE GRASS

COLOR: green
SIZE: 1 foot tall

Like Eelgrass, **Turtle Grass** grows underwater. It looks similar but its blades are wider than Eelgrass blades. Also, Turtle Grass lives where the ocean is warmer, in the Florida Keys and on the Gulf of Florida. Turtle Grass and Eelgrass never grow in the same place. Many sea creatures make their home in Turtle Grass.

MANGROVE TREE

These plants grow in ocean bays and swamps of Florida. They have shiny, leathery leaves. There are three different kinds of mangrove trees. They look similar but not exactly alike. The place where they grow can help you identify them.

BLACK MANGROVE

SIZE: 10 to 40 feet tall

The **Black Mangrove** grows closer to shore, behind the Red Mangrove. Its leaves are fuzzy and the flowers are white.

132

Red Mangrove

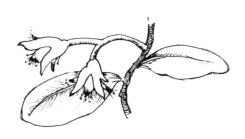

Size: up to 20 feet tall

The **Red Mangrove** grows farthest out in the water. Its green, leathery leaves have black dots underneath. The flowers are pale yellow.

White Mangrove

Size: 20 to 40 feet tall

The **White Mangrove** also has white flowers, but its leaves are shiny and leathery. They live in tidal swamps.

133

AMERICAN BEACH GRASS

COLOR: green
SIZE: 2 to 4 feet tall

This is the most common plant on the beaches and dunes of the Atlantic Coast. It is also one of the most important. Its strong, deep roots connect under the sand, helping to keep the sand from blowing away. **American Beach Grass** is tall, and its stem is strong and flat.

SEA OATS

COLOR: green
SIZE: 3 to 6 feet tall

From Virginia to Florida, **Sea Oats** grows on the dunes with American Beach Grass. Sea Oats is a taller plant, and it has large flower clusters at the top that look like the tail feathers of an ostrich.

REED GRASS

COLOR: green
SIZE: 10 to 12 feet tall

This is the tallest grass on the Atlantic Coast. It stands ten to twelve feet tall and grows in large colonies in slat marshes. Walking or riding past a salt marsh, you can see the fat cluster of seeds at the top of the **Reed Grass**, and you can hear the soft rustling sound it makes when the wind blows.

SALTMARSH BULLRUSH

SIZE: 4 to 6 feet tall

You may see **Saltmarsh Bullrush** near Reed Grass, but it is shorter and has long, sharp leaves. In the summer and fall, you can see brown, oval seeds in bunches where the leaf grows out of the stem.

135

SALTMARSH CORDGRASS

SIZE: 2 to 8 feet tall

Although their names are similar, this cordgrass looks different from Saltmeadow Cordgrass. **Saltmarsh Cordgrass** is twice as tall, and it grows closely together in groups in the mud of marshes or saltwater riverbanks. It has wider leaves than Saltmeadow Cordgrass, and its flower is white.

You can see huge fields of **Saltmeadow Cordgrass** grass in salt marshes. It is easy to identify because it doesn't stand tall as other grasses do. It looks flattened, as if large animals have been lying on it. But it is really the wind that flattens Saltmeadow Cordgrass, which bends over easily because of its thin stem. It can grow to be three feet tall, but it is hard to tell its height since the grass is lying down. In late summer, Saltmeadow Cordgrass has purple flowers at the top of its blades.

Saltmeadow Cordgrass

Size: 1 to 3 feet tall

Spike Grass

Size: 1 to 2 feet tall

Spike Grass is a shorter grass that grows in higher spots in salt marshes. It has a tough stem with flat, pointed leaves. In late summer and early fall it has a light green cluster of flowers at the top of the stem.

A relative of the cactus, **Glasswort** is a tough little plant with a thick stem and many branches. These branches are green in the summer and bright red or brown in the fall. They look like many short pieces of branches hooked together like sausage links. This plant feels rubbery when you touch it. Like the cactus, Glasswort doesn't need much water, and it can store water in its branches. It grows in salty, sandy dirt near salt marshes and beaches.

GLASS WORT

SIZE: 12 inches tall

SEA LAVENDER

SIZE: 1 to 2 feet tall

Sea Lavender and Glasswort are often seen growing together along the edge of a salt marsh. Like Glasswort, Sea Lavender has many branches. The two plants are often the same height, although in some places, Sea Lavender can be two feet tall. And they are different in other ways. Sea Lavender is not related to cactus. In the summertime, many tiny, delicate, lavender flowers grow on the branches of the Sea Lavender, which is how this plant got its name. Sea Lavender has tiny, green leaves that are shaped like little spoons. There are several large leaves at the bottom of the plant.

Sea Rocket

Size: 6 to 18 inches tall

In some places on the Atlantic Coast, this is the only plant you will see growing right on the beach. **Sea Rocket** is tough enough to live in the salty sand, and its thick, rubbery leaves can hold water, just as the leaves of a cactus can. It also grows on dunes. Sea Rocket is named for the shape of the green seedpods that grow on the plant. In the summer, it has light blue or lavender flowers.

Dusty Miller

Size: 2 feet tall

It is easy to identify this plant. The light green leaves of **Dusty Miller** are covered with tiny white hairs that make the plant look as if it is covered with dust. These little hairs help protect the plant from both hot sun and cold weather. Dusty Miller does not grow in bunches. You often see many single plants growing on the dunes and along the edge of a beach. In summer, Dusty Miller has a bright yellow flower. It blooms on the top of a stalk that grows out of the top of the plant.

BEACH HEATHER

SIZE: 8 to 12 inches tall

This plant looks like a little bush. It is less than a foot tall and grows in groups along beaches and sand dunes. You can see from the little mounds of sand at the bottom of the plants that **Beach Heather** roots help hold the sand in place. Beach Heather has small, green, fuzzy leaves. For a short time in late spring or early summer, Beach Heather is covered with tiny, bright yellow flowers.

140

SEASIDE GOLDENROD

SIZE: 2 to 8 feet tall

This plant stands tall along the dunes and on the edges of salt marshes. It can be eight feet tall. Sometimes it is only two feet tall, but it is almost always taller than the other flowering plants growing around it. Often you see many **Seaside Goldenrod** plants growing together. They have long, pointed, green leaves. This plant is easiest to identify from early summer to late fall, when clusters of golden yellow flowers grow on top of the stem.

BEACH PEA

SIZE: 2 to 3 feet tall

The **Beach Pea** looks a lot like the pea plant that grows in vegetable gardens. It is a viny plant that trails along the dunes and climbs up and around other plants. Green

141

leaves grow in pairs from stems that are attached to the plant's main stem. The ends of the leaf stems curl like little pigs' tails. It is these curly little ends, called tendrils, that wind around dune grasses and other plants. They also help hold the plant in place. The Beach Pea has delicate pink or purple flowers all summer long. Its seedpods look like the seedpods of its cousin, the garden pea, and they are good to eat. Many birds and small animals, and some people, eat the seedpods.

BEACH ROSE

SIZE: 3 to 6 feet tall

This wild rose has many names: Sea Rose, Salt-spray Rose, and Wrinkled Rose. It is a bush with many woody branches. You will often find many **Beach Rose** bushes growing together in thick hedges. These hedges are sometimes six feet tall. Beautiful pink and white flowers with yellow centers bloom on Beach Rose stems all summer long. Be careful if you pick one. The stems are covered

142

BAYBERRY

SIZE: 1 $\frac{1}{2}$ to 6 feet tall

with sharp thorns. In the fall and winter, the Beach Rose has round, red seedpods the size of a large marble. These seedpods are the fruit of the Beach Rose. They are called *rose hips*. They are good to eat. Sometimes people use them to make jelly or tea.

Like the Beach Rose, **Bayberry** is a bush with woody stems. Its dark-green leaves have a wonderful smell. You may have smelled Bayberry in your kitchen. Bay leaves are used to flavor soups, pasta, and other foods. Bayberry has no flower that you can see, but in the summer and fall, it has bunches of grayish white berries growing on its stems. These berries are covered with wax and are not good to eat. From New Jersey to Florida, you might see a close relative of the Bayberry, called Wax Myrtle. The two plants look alike, but Wax Myrtle can be as tall as a tree.

FIND THESE FASCINATING FACTS

- What animals need estuaries for a nursery?
- What kind of trees have breathing holes in their roots?
- What did some farmers do 200 years ago that damaged estuarine wetlands?

7 Estuaries: Where Rivers Meet the Sea

When many people think of the seashore, they picture a sandy beach or a rocky coast next to the open ocean. But there is another kind of shoreline landscape and it is just as interesting. It is the *estuary*. Estuaries are where freshwater rivers and streams from the land flow into the salty ocean. (The ocean itself is not part of an estuary.)

Estuaries can be quite different from each other depending upon where they are located and what type of land is around them. A river, cove, inlet, or *bayou* can be considered an estuary, as long as it meets and flows into the salty seawater. Estuaries can be surrounded by *wetlands* (marshes and *tidal flats*), *barrier islands,* or reefs. There are estuaries in the wilderness, in the country, and even in the city.

One important thing that estuaries have in common is that they are protected from the open ocean and its waves, currents, and winds. Also, like the ocean, all estuaries are affected by the tides. When the tide is high, an estuary is deep and the wetlands surrounding it are mostly under water. At low tide, an estuary is very shallow, and the wetlands are exposed to the sun and wind. Because of the tides and the mixture of freshwater and saltwater, estuaries are constantly changing. All of these things create a unique habitat for many plants and animals.

Most estuaries are muddy or sandy on the bottom. As freshwater flows into the ocean, it slows down. Sand and dirt, called *sediment*, that collected in and floated down the river as it moved through the land, sinks to the bottom, creating the perfect muddy habitat for many worms and shellfish. Estuaries are a "nursery," or breeding ground, for many kinds of fish. (More than two-thirds of the fish and shellfish that humans eat spend at least part of their lives in an estuary.)

Estuaries and the wetlands around them also provide homes and feeding grounds for birds. The birds make their nests in the marsh grasses and feast on the many worms, fish, and tiny sea creatures that live in the neighborhood.

On the central and southern coasts of Florida, the estuarine ecosystem includes mangrove swamps. A mangrove is a type of tropical tree that has adapted itself to life in tidal waters. Mangrove trees have large root systems that look like a tangle of arms and legs; these special roots keep the trees propped up out of the water. Part of the roots stay above water even at high tide, and they have many tiny "breathing" holes that work like snorkels to supply air (oxygen) for the tree. These trees provide habitat for many animals, including birds.

Estuarine wetlands play another important role in the environment. When there is a storm that makes the ocean very high, the wetlands act like a sponge, absorbing the "extra" seawater and helping to prevent flooding of lands nearby. The estuarine ecosystem also helps to filter out pollutants, such as harmful chemicals in fertilizer, which travel in rivers and streams from *cultivated* lands, such as farms and golf courses, to the open ocean.

All along the Atlantic Coast, estuaries and wetlands have been damaged and, in some places, destroyed by development. Two hundred years ago, farmers in New England used salt hay from the marshes to feed their animals. They dug ditches and built dams to block the tidal seawater, creating large pastures. (In some salt marshes, you can still see these ditches.) Some estuarine areas were drained to get rid of mosquito breeding grounds. Others have been drained and filled with dirt so that houses could be built there. Scientists say that by the 1950s, about half of all estuaries on the Atlantic Coast had been changed by human activities.

In the 1960s, scientists and others began to realize the importance of estuaries and wetlands. Now there are many programs and groups working to help protect estuarine areas from further damage, and even to restore the health of some estuaries and wetlands. The National Estuarine Research Reserve System (NERRS) was established in 1972 by the United States Congress. At many NERRS sites around the United States, scientists and ecologists study the estuaries—there is still much to learn.

Appendix B lists the NERRS's East Coast reserves. Many of the reserves have wooden walkways near estuaries, or even over wetlands, allowing visitors a closer view without harming the environment. Don't forget to take your binoculars to these places. One of the most exciting ways to experience an estuary is from the water, in a small boat, such as a rowboat, canoe, or kayak. You can't do this at low tide, of course, when there is very little wa-

Estuaries are dynamic wildlife areas

ter in an estuary. But at high tide, and even between tides, this is an exciting way to explore the fascinating estuarine world. It's very important to use a tide chart when planning such a trip. Traveling up an estuary by boat, away from the ocean, you could get stranded in the mud when the tide goes out.

Many of the estuarine reserves listed in Appendix B have educational centers where you can learn more about this fascinating coastal environment. Most offer guided tours as well. There is a lot of information about estuaries on the Internet, too. (See "Appendix A: Sea-Searching on the Internet.") The more people learn about estuaries, the easier it will be to protect them now and in the future.

Appendix A ✴
Sea-Searching on the Internet

There are many websites with interesting information about the ocean and about plant and animal life in the sea and on the coast. Here are just a few to get you started. Most have links to many other sites as well.

www.mos.org/oceans

This cool site, called "Oceans Alive!," is all about the ocean. Click on "Resources" to find fun projects about ocean science and a reading list for kids. Also, under Resources, you'll find links to other interesting websites. For instance, if you click on the link called "Secrets of the Ocean Realm," you can download a screensaver that will turn your computer screen into an aquarium. Or click on the link to the Woods Hole Oceanographic Institution, then go to "Dive and Discover" (scroll down on the home page) to see what scientists are studying currently.

capelookoutstudies.org

The Cape Lookout (North Carolina) Studies Program is an environmental education, research, and *conservation* program sponsored by the North Carolina Maritime Museum with the Cape Lookout National Seashore. This site has information about dolphins, sea turtles, birds, renewable energy, and much more. The Field Guide's pages have dozens of color photographs of seashore birds, plants, and shells. On the Fin Game page you can try identifying dolphins from photos of their fins.

www.oceanconservancy.org

The Ocean Conservancy works to protect ocean ecosystems. On this site, you can learn what this group is doing and why. There is lots of information about endangered marine life, such as monk seals, manatees, and sharks. In the Fish and Wildlife section, click on "Sea Turtles" to download a free coloring book.

www.epa.gov/owow/oceans/kids.html

This site is hosted by the U.S. Environmental Protection Agency. Start on "Oceans and Coasts for Children, Students, and Teachers" and you'll find great stuff for kids. There are quizzes, games, coloring books to download, and links to other interesting websites.

www.epa.gov/owow/estuaries/kids

The U.S. Environmental Protection Agency developed this Web site to introduce kids to the *ecology* of the estuaries. "Exploring Estuaries" includes virtual tours of some fascinating estuaries. Teachers will find some creative ideas for lessons and activities.

www.nerrs.noaa.gov

The National Estuarine Research Reserve System hosts this site. You will find information about estuaries and research reserves on the East Coast (and elsewhere in the United States). Look here to find the estuary that is closest to where you live.

www.lobster.org

Hosted by the Lobster Conservancy, this site includes everything you might ever want to know about lobsters. There are some interesting drawings that show how they live, grow, and molt.

www.horseshoecrab.org

Horseshoe crabs are so important—they have been on Earth for more than 350 million years!—that there is a research group devoted to studying them. That group hosts this Web site, packed with information about this fascinating creature, including its history, evolution, conservation, and the horseshoe crab's important role in the field of medicine. Click on "Anatomy" to learn about all of its body parts. On the page called "Get Involved," you can find out how to help protect the animals, how to report where you have seen a horseshoe crab, and how to enter the annual horseshoe crab arts contest (poems, stories, and images) for children in kindergarten through 12th grade.

www.birds.cornell.edu/AllAboutBirds/

If you are interested in birds, you will love this site. Hosted by the Cornell Lab of *Ornithology*, this site tells how to begin the hobby of bird watching, best birding places throughout the United States, and how to attract birds to your backyard. Perhaps most impressive, though, is the Bird Guide section. Click on "Species Accounts" and you will find hundreds of birds listed in alphabetical order. For each species there is a page with a photograph, descriptions of the bird and its habitat, conservation status, "cool facts," and a map showing its range (where it lives). You can even listen to the sound that each bird makes.

www.baldeagleinfo.com

The ornithological symbol of our nation and the only eagle that is unique to North America (this is the only part of the world where it lives) deserves to have its own website. This site is filled with information about the Bald Eagle's history, habits, nests, migration, and much more. There is a page of legends, myths, and even a page of poems about this enormous raptor. Be sure to click on "Old Abe" to read about a legendary Bald Eagle that served as a mascot for a military regiment. There are spectacular Bald Eagle photographs that you can download free to use as screen savers for your computer. All the photographs are by Hope Rutledge, who created and owns the website.

www.noamkelp.com

This site is about a kelp company in Maine, but it offers a lot of general information about seaweed and several recipes for cooking with seaweed. At the bottom of the Home Page, click on "Seaweed Field Guide."

APPENDIX B ⚝

NATURAL AREAS TO EXPLORE ALONG THE ATLANTIC COAST

You might already have some favorite places to visit when you go to the seashore. But part of the fun of exploring is finding new places. Here is a list of some special parks and nature reserves along the Atlantic Coast. The outdoor places listed below are for everyone to enjoy. Some charge a fee to visit; many do not.

Some places are small; some are very large. Most have hiking trails along a beach, through salt marshes, sand dunes, seaside forests, or over rocks. Some have exhibits and programs about the environment.

The natural areas are listed alphabetically under the state in which they are found. If no town name is included, it means that the natural area spreads across several towns or has more than one site. You can find out more about each place when you visit the area. Many of these natural areas can be found on the Internet. websites include information such as directions, wildlife you might see, facilities, and types of recreation that are available.

CONNECTICUT

Barn Island Wildlife Management Area, Stonington
Bluff Point State Park and Reserve, Groton
Coastal Center at Milford Point, Milford
Hammonasset Beach State Park, Madison

DELAWARE

Beach Plum Island State Park, Broadkill Beach
Bombay Hook National Wildlife Reserve, Smyrna
Cape Henlopen State Park, Lewes
Delaware National Estuarine Research Reserve, Dover
Delaware Seashore State Park, Rehoboth Beach
Prime Hook National Wildlife Refuge, Milton
Woodland Beach Wildlife Area, Smyrna

FLORIDA

Bahia Honda State Park, Bahia Honda Key
Biscayne National Park, Homestead
Canaveral National Seashore, Titusville
Collier-Seminole State Park, Naples
The Conservancy's Briggs Nature Center, Naples
Darling National Wildlife Refuge, Sanibel
Everglades National Park, Homestead
Fort Clinch State Park, Fernandina Beach
Fort DeSoto Park, Tierra Verde
Guana River State Park, South Ponte
Guana Tolomato Matanzas National Estuarine Research
    Reserve, St. Augustine
Gulf Islands National Seashore, Gulf Breeze
John D. MacArthur Beach State Park, North Palm Beach
John Pennekamp Coral Reef State Park, Key Largo
Key Largo Hammocks State Botanical Site, Key Largo
Little Talbot Island State Park, Jacksonville
Loxahatchee National Wildlife Refuge, Boynton Beach
Merritt Island National Wildlife Refuge, Titusville

Rookery Bay National Estuarine Research Reserve, Naples
Six Mile Cypress Preserve, Fort Myers
St. Joseph Peninsula State Park, St. Joseph Peninsula
St. Mark's National Wildlife Refuge, St. Marks

GEORGIA

Jekyll Island State Park, Jekyll Island
Savannah National Wildlife Refuge, Savannah
Skidaway Island State Park, Savannah

MAINE

Acadia National Park, Mt. Desert Island
East Point Sanctuary, Biddeford
Ferry Beach State Park, Saco
Goose Rocks Beach, Kennebunkport
Pemaquid Beach Park, Bristol
Petit Manan National Wildlife Refuge, East Steuben
Popham Beach State Park, Phippsburg
Prout's Neck Bird Sanctuary, Scarborough
Quoddy Head State Park, Lubec
Rachel Carson National Wildlife Refuge, Wells
Reid State Park, Georgetown
Scarborough Wildlife Management Area, Scarborough
Two Lights State Park, Cape Elizabeth
Wells National Estuarine Research Reserve, Wells
Wolfe's Neck Woods State Park, Freeport

MARYLAND

Assateague Island National Seashore
Calvert Cliffs State Park
Chesapeake Bay National Estuarine Research Reserve
Eastern Neck National Wildlife Reserve, Rock Hall
Elk Neck State Park, North East
Jug Bay Natural Area, Upper Marlboro

Point Lookout State Park, Scotland
Sandy Point State Park, Annapolis

MASSACHUSETTS

Cape Cod National Seashore
Crane's Beach, Ipswich
Halibut Point Reservation, Rockport
Ipswich River Wildlife Sanctuary, Topsfield
Parker River National Wildlife Refuge, Newburyport
Salisbury Beach State Reservation, Salisbury Beach
Waquoit Bay National Estuarine Research Reserve, Waquoit
Wellfleet Bay Wildlife Sanctuary, South Wellfleet
World's End Reservation, Hingham

NEW HAMPSHIRE

Great Bay National Estuarine Research Reserve,
    Greenland
Hampton Beach State Park, Hampton Beach

NEW JERSEY

Brigantine National Wildlife Refuge, Oceanville
Cape May Bird Observatory, Cape May
Cape May Point State Park, Cape May
Fortescue Wildlife Management Area
Gateway National Recreational Area
Island Beach State Park, Seaside Park
Jacques Cousteau National Estuarine Research Reserve,
    Tuckerton
Stone Harbor Point, Stone Harbor

NEW YORK

Caumsett State Park, Lloyd Neck
Fire Island National Seashore, Long Island
Hudson River National Estuarine Research Reserve

Jamaica Bay Wildlife Refuge, Brooklyn/Queens
Montauk Point State Park, Montauk
Orient Beach State Park, Orient

North Carolina

Cape Hatteras National Seashore
Jockey's Ridge State Park, Nags Head
North Inlet-Winyah Bay National Estuarine Research Reserve,
    Georgetown

Rhode Island

Beavertail Point State Park, Jamestown
Burlingame State Park, Charlestown
Napatree Point, Watch Hill
Narragansett Bay National Estuarine Research Reserve,
    Prudence Island
Ninigret National Wildlife Refuge, Charlestown
Norman Bird Sanctuary, Middletown
Trustom Pond, South Kingston

South Carolina

Ace Basin National Estuarine Research Reserve, Charleston
Cape Romain National Wildlife Refuge, Awendaw
Hunting Island State Park, Beaufort

Virginia

Assateague Island National Seashore
Back Bay National Wildlife Refuge, Oceana
Chesapeake Bay National Estuarine Research Reserve
Mason Neck National Wildlife Refuge, Lorton
Ragged Island Wildlife Management Area, Newport News
Seashore State Park, Virginia Beach
Westmoreland State Park, Montross

GLOSSARY

algae A primitive plant that has no real stems, roots, or leaves. Seaweed is a kind of alga.

antenna A small (sometimes long) thin animal part attached to the animal's head. Like a cat's whisker, the antenna helps the animal to "feel" or sense its surroundings. An animal that has an antenna always has two of them. The word for more than one antenna is antennae.

barrier island A strip of sand that lies parallel to the seashore.

bay In a lake or the ocean, a bay is a place along the shore where the water is quiet and protected from the wind and waves. A bay is sometimes called a cove or an inlet.

bayou A marshy river found in the southern part of the United States.

bed A group of sea creatures, such as mussels, that live together attached to rocks, mud, and each other. A bed of mussels is sometimes called a colony of mussels.

bird sanctuary An outdoor place where birds are protected by law from hunters who might disturb either the birds or their nests.

camouflage On an animal, coloring that helps it blend in with its environment. Camouflage helps an animal hide from other animals that might want to eat it.

climate The weather conditions, such as temperature and amount of rainfall, that are typical in a particular area.

colony A group of animals or plants living together. Barnacles and mussels live in colonies, sometimes called beds.

concentric Lines that run in parallel circles around the same center.

conservation Preservation of the natural environment.

cove Another word for a bay or inlet.

cultivate To prepare soil for growing vegetables, fruits, or other crops or for creating a particular kind of grassy surface such as a lawn, a golf course, or an athletic field. Cultivation involves breaking up the soil and sometimes adding chemicals to help the crops grow.

current The movement or flow of water in a particular direction. Air also moves in currents.

dune A hill of sand that was made by the wind.

ecology The study of the relationship between plants and animals and their environment.

ecosystem A community of plants, animals, and nonliving things, such as rocks and sand.

erosion The wearing away of the earth's surface. Erosion is often caused by water or wind.

estuary An area where a freshwater river enters the sea.

eyespot A spot on an animal that senses light or dark, but cannot see as a human eye can.

eyestalk A stalk-like body part that sits on top of the head of a crab or other creature. The animal's eye is on top of the eyestalk.

field mark On a bird, the color of its feathers or of a body part. Field marks help people identify birds.

fin A thin body part on a fish that helps it to swim.

fragile Easy to break.

gill The body part that allows some water creatures to breathe. Animals that have gills take oxygen from the water, just as animals with lungs take oxygen from the air.

growth lines Curved lines or ridges on a mollusk that show how the mollusk has grown. Growth lines on a mollusk are like growth rings on a tree.

habitat The particular place where a plant or animal lives. For example, the rocky ocean floor is the habitat for the American Lobster.

high-tide line The place on the shore where the water is highest when the tide is in.

hinge On a two-shelled mollusk, the place where the two shells are attached.

holdfast The part of a seaweed that attaches the seaweed to a rock or a shell. The holdfast on seaweed is like the root of a land plant.

inlet Another word for a cove or bay.

larva The young form of an animal after it has hatched from an egg and before it is an adult. Butterflies, frogs, and barnacles are some animals that begin life as a larva. Sometimes the larva looks like a tiny worm.

low-tide line The place on the shore where the water is lowest when the tide is out.

marsh Land that is flat and partly covered with water. A marsh has plants, usually tall grass, growing around and in it. A salt marsh is a marsh that is near or connected to the ocean. The saltwater of a salt marsh rises and falls with the tides.

migrate To move from one place to another as the seasons of the year change. Many birds and some ocean-living animals migrate.

mollusk A water animal that has a soft body covered by a hard shell.

molt The process of an animal shedding its outer covering—shell, hair, or feathers—while growing or renewing that outer covering.

muscle scar The mark on the inside of a two-shelled mollusk that shows where the foot, or muscle, was once attached.

organism An individual plant of animal consisting of one cell or a group of cells or parts.

ornithology The scientific study of birds.

pesticide A chemical used to kill insects and rodents. Farmers use pesticides to protect their gardens, but pesticides can harm or kill other animals, too.

pincer The grabbing claw of an animal, such as a crab or lobster.

predator An animal that eats another animal.

prey An animal that is eaten by another animal.

raptor A bird of prey, such as an owl, a hawk, an osprey, or an eagle.

reef A ridge of rock or coral that lies just under the surface of the ocean.

regenerate To replace a body part that has been destroyed or removed. Starfish can regenerate rays (arms) and lobsters can regenerate claws.

ribs The lines or ridges on the outside of shells.

rose hip The seedpod, or fruit, of the Beach Rose.

sediment Sand or soil that settles to the bottom of a body of water.

species A group of living things that have similar characteristics and appearance. On planet Earth, scientists have identified and named more than 287,600 plant species and about 1,250,000 animal species.

Spire A word used to describe the pointed top of a one-shelled mollusk, such as conch or whelk.

Staircase shells Another name for a shell called the Angulate Wentletrap. The shell is shaped something like a winding staircase.

surf Ocean waves that crash, or "break," on the shore.

tentacle A body part that a water animal uses to grab food or to hold on to objects. Jellyfish and sea anemones are among the animals that have tentacles.

tidal flats Muddy areas around estuaries that are covered by seawater at high tide and exposed at low tide. They are covered with grass and provide homes for many plants and animals.

tide chart A list that shows when the tide will be high and when the tide will be low.

tide pool A pool of seawater left in the rocks or sand when the tide goes out.

tides The rising and falling of the ocean that takes place twice each day. The tides are caused by the changing position of the earth in relation to the sun and moon.

toxic The quality of being poisonous.

translucent Somewhat transparent, but not as transparent as clear glass.

undertow Water current that moves back toward the open sea when waves break on the shore. Sometimes undertow is very strong and dangerous. It can knock you down and pull you out into the deep water.

venomous Poisonous or toxic.

Wentletrap The Dutch word for winding staircase.

wetlands Marshes, swamps, or other damp areas of land.

whorl On a seashell, a spiral turn around the shell.

CHECKLIST

As you see each plant, animal, and shell, make a checkmark on the list below. Within each group, the names are listed in alphabetical order. The page numbers show where to find each plant or animal in this guidebook. You might want to write down where you found each one. For example, you could name the state, town, beach, or park. When you have checked off everything on the list, cut out the Sea-Searcher's Award and hang it on the wall or put it in your scrapbook.

	PAGE	WHERE FOUND
SEA CREATURES		
❑ American Lobster	16	_____
Barnacle		
❑ Bay Barnacle	31	_____
❑ Ivory Barnacle	32	_____
❑ Large Rock Barnacle	32	_____
❑ Little Gray Barnacle	32	_____
❑ Northern Rock Barnacle	33	_____
❑ Big-Eyed Beach Flea	30	_____
Chiton		
❑ Common Eastern Chiton	37	_____
❑ Red Northern Chiton	37	_____

CHECKLIST ～～～～～～～～～～～～～～～～

	PAGE	WHERE FOUND
❑ Limulus Leech	47	_____
❑ Two-Gilled Blood Worm	47	_____

SHELLS TO COLLECT

	PAGE	WHERE FOUND
❑ Alphabet Cone	69	_____
❑ Angel Wing	75	_____
❑ Angulate Wentletrap	68	_____
❑ Apple Murex	67	_____
❑ Atlantic Dogwhinkle	55	_____
❑ Atlantic Oyster Drill	55	_____
❑ Bleeding Tooth	64	_____
❑ Blood Ark	76	_____
❑ Buttercup Lucine	73	_____
❑ Chestnut Turban	60	_____
Clam		
❑ Atlantic Jackknife Clam	80	_____
❑ Atlantic Nut Clam	80	_____
❑ Atlantic Razor Clam	81	_____
❑ Atlantic Surf Clam	81	_____
❑ File Yoldia	82	_____
❑ Soft-Shell Clam	82	_____
Cockle Shell		
❑ Giant Atlantic Cockle	77	_____
❑ Morton's Cockle	77	_____
❑ Northern Dwarf Cockle	78	_____
❑ Strawberry Cockle	78	_____
❑ Yellow Cockle	79	_____
❑ Common American Auger	69	_____
❑ Common American Sundial	67	_____

	PAGE	WHERE FOUND

SHOREBIRDS

❑ American Black Duck — 112 — _____

❑ Bald Eagle — 117 — _____

❑ Bufflehead — 114 — _____

❑ Canada Goose — 115 — _____

❑ Common Loon — 110 — _____

❑ Double-Crested Cormorant — 109 — _____

❑ Great Blue Heron — 96 — _____

❑ Great White Egret — 97 — _____

Gull

  ❑ Great Black-Backed Gull — 105 — _____

  ❑ Herring Gull — 105 — _____

  ❑ Laughing Gull — 106 — _____

❑ Mallard — 111 — _____

❑ Osprey — 116 — _____

Pelican

  ❑ American White Pelican — 107 — _____

  ❑ Brown Pelican — 108 — _____

❑ Red-Winged Blackbird — 118 — _____

Sandpiper

  ❑ Least Sandpiper — 99 — _____

  ❑ Purple Sandpiper — 100 — _____

  ❑ Sanderling — 100 — _____

  ❑ Semipalmated Sandpiper — 101 — _____

  ❑ Spotted Sandpiper — 101 — _____

❑ Seaside Sparrow — 119 — _____

❑ Snowy Egret — 98 — _____

	Page	Where Found
Tern		
❏ Caspian Tern	102	_____
❏ Common Tern	103	_____
❏ Forster's Tern	103	_____
❏ Roseate Tern	104	_____
Seashore Plants		
In the Sea		
❏ Chenille Weed	129	_____
❏ Dulse	125	_____
❏ Green Thread Algae	122	_____
❏ Irish Moss	129	_____
❏ Kelp	124	_____
❏ Knotted Wrack	124	_____
❏ Link Confetti	128	_____
❏ Purple Laver	127	_____
❏ Rockweed	123	_____
❏ Sea Colander	126	_____
❏ Sea Grass	128	_____
❏ Sea Lettuce	127	_____
❏ Sea Potato	130	_____
Near the Sea		
❏ American Beach Grass	134	_____
❏ Bayberry	143	_____
❏ Beach Heather	140	_____
❏ Beach Pea	141	_____
❏ Beach Rose	142	_____
❏ Dusty Miller	139	_____

ABOUT THE AUTHOR

JUDITH HANSEN grew up in Maine's Lincoln County and has spent many hours exploring the coastal and inland waterways of the Northeast. A graduate of the University of Maine, she taught primary school in Boston and in Williamsburg, Virginia; nature study always figured prominently in her classroom activities. Ms. Hansen began her writing career in 1972, working variously as a journalist, freelance writer, publicist, and marketing communications consultant over the next ten years. She now lives in Kennebunk, Maine, where she publishes *The Tourist News*, a three-season arts and entertainment newspaper. *Seashells in My Pocket* is her first book.

ABOUT THE ARTIST

DONNA SABAKA majored in Fine Arts at Bowling Green State University in Ohio, and has studied at the Cleveland Art Institute and the University of Southern Maine. Her illustrations have appeared in several books for children and adults. As a watercolorist, she specializes in florals and seascapes. Ms. Sabaka lives in Arundel, Maine, and has exhibited her work in several galleries and in many local and regional shows.

INDEX

177

Sea Searcher's Award

PRINT YOUR NAME HERE

Has found and identified all the animals, shells, described and illustrated in *Seashells in My Pocket*

DATE